THE NAKED TRUTH ABOUT SEX

HOW TO DEVELOP MORE INTIMACY INSIDE AND OUTSIDE THE BEDROOM

ASHLEY WILLIS

DAVE WILLIS

XO
PUBLISHING

©2017 Dave and Ashley Willis

The Naked Truth About Sex

Marriage Today™

PO Box 59888

Dallas, Texas 75229

1-800-380-6330

marriagetoday.com

XO Publishing

Printed in the United States of America

CONTENTS

INTRODUCTION

God created sex.

Think about that for a second! Maybe you've had some common-but-misguided views of God where He is cold or distant or out-of-touch, and He's looking down on anybody who's having a good time. When you think about sex (which you probably do all the time), you might visualize God shaking His head in disappointment or disgust, but He's the one who thought of it first! Everything good in the world is something God thought of first.

God in all of His wisdom could've been fine without making the Human Race in the first place. Even after making mankind, He could have made us asexual beings that just spawned more humans without needing any sex at all. He chose to create sex. He chose to make it pleasurable. He chose to make it awesome! That's something to be thankful for!

In fact, next Thanksgiving, when your family is going around the table listing reasons to be thankful, you should be the one to speak up and say, "God, I want to thank you for something we're all thankful for but nobody wants to say it in front of Grandma... Thank you for making sex! It's awesome. Let's eat some turkey."

Grandma will probably even shout an, "Amen!"

Perhaps one of the reasons why we get uneasy talking about sexuality is because sex isn't always a positive experience. Sex is certainly a wonderful gift, but sometimes it gets misused, misplaced or misunderstood.

When that happens, emotional pain replaces physical pleasure and baggage finds its way into the bedroom. Whether we realize it or not, we all have some form of baggage related to sex.

Some sexual baggage has to do with past regrets. When we've made sexual choices that were out-of-bounds from God's original and perfect design for sex, it creates a visual reel in our brains full of images we wish we could erase. Sometimes baggage comes from being raised with an unhealthy view of sex that misrepresented what sexual intimacy was all about and it created misguided views or unrealistic expectations.

Some baggage happens because of past abuse. These wounds can be the deepest and most painful of them all. A staggering number of people have been abused, molested, objectified or mistreated in a way that leaves deep scars.

Sex was never intended to be used as a weapon to hurt others or as a lust-fueled form of self-gratification at the expense of others. Lust looks at people as objects to be used; love looks at people as souls to be cherished. When lust wins out, people get hurt.

So many of us are carrying scars as a result of these intimate and invisible wounds. Whether the wounds came from our own choices or from becoming the victim of someone else's choices, these wounds can seep into a marriage and cause distrust, disunity and discouragement.

If you're currently struggling to connect with your spouse inside and/or outside the bedroom, please know that things can get better.

The simple fact that you're reading this book right now proves that you're willing to take action to make things better, and the truths and tools you'll discover on the coming pages can help you get to a healthier and more fulfilling place in your sex life and your overall relationship with your spouse. Regardless of where you currently are on the spectrum of marital health and passionate lovemaking (or lack of it), this book can help you.

The Unique Format of this Book

We've written several marriage books, but this one is unique for several reasons. First of all, it's our first book focused primarily on issues related to sexual intimacy in marriage. We receive countless messages and questions through our websites and social media channels, and an overwhelming number of those messages and questions have to do sex.

We don't claim to be "experts" about sex, but we do feel a deep sense of responsibility to start conversations about healthy sexuality in marriage that will help married couples grow in this important area of marriage while also reclaiming God's original and beautiful intent for sex from a culture that has attempted to hijack and redefine sex on its own terms.

This book is also unique because of its format. We connect with millions of readers through our blogs, and we've found that a blog-type format seems to resonate with people because those articles are relatively succinct, to-the-point and they usually include a short list of actionable items that help the reader put the content into practical use right away.

Instead of typical "chapters" like you'll find in most our other books, *The Naked Truth about Sex* is a collection of "articles" focused on specific issues related to sex and intimacy within marriage.

You may choose to read every chapter in sequential order like you would with a traditional book, or you might prefer to use this book as a quick reference guide where you can use the Table of Contents to focus on the questions and issues most pertinent to your specific needs, desires, circumstances and questions.

However you choose to use this book, we hope that the content you'll find on the coming pages will bring renewed passion to your faith, your marriage and your sex life (and yes, all three of those things are intimately interconnected).

A Brief Introduction about Us

Since we're going to be sharing about such intimate topics in this book, it seems fitting to introduce ourselves so you know who we are. There will be some stories from our own lives and marriage throughout the book, but this book certainly isn't about us. It's about YOU. It's about equipping you and your spouse with the tools every couple needs to build a rock-solid marriage and a thriving sex life together.

Simply to give you some context as you read, we are Dave and Ashley Willis. We have a shared passion for encouraging and helping other married couples to grow in their faith and in their relationship with each other. We don't take ourselves too seriously, but we don't take our work lightly.

We believe that building a strong marriage is one of the most important and sacred tasks you'll ever do. It will have an immeasurable impact on your life, your legacy and your family.

We both wrote this book in partnership, but just to make it an easier reading experience for you, we tried to write with one voice. This means that whenever possible, we'll use "I" instead of "We" and we won't clarify which one of us is speaking unless it's a personal story and you'll need that information for context (i.e. "I (Dave) have a friend who asked me for marriage advice" or "I (Ashley) remember the first time one of my friends faced a marriage crisis").

For those of you who have already been part of our online communities, thank you for your ongoing prayers, encouragement and support! It's such an honor to be connected to you and we deeply appreciate your feedback and you taking the time to share our quotes, videos and articles with your friends online. Together, we are partnered with you in helping build stronger marriages and families!

For those of you who aren't currently connected to any of our websites or online communities, we'd love to connect with you. At the end of the book there's an "About the Authors" section with multiple websites where you can learn more. We'd love to hear your feedback as you read this book, so if you have questions or thoughts you'd like to share with us at any point, please email us at: DaveWillis@mar-riagetoday.com or AshleyWillis@marriagetoday.com -

We'd love to hear from you!

A Few Final Instructions

As you read this book, you're most likely going to feel a mixture of emotions. You might find yourself nodding your head in agreement feeling affirmed by some of the things you're doing right in your sex life.

There might be other moments when the true stories (with names and identities changed to protect everyone's anonymity) will open your eyes to the magnitude of struggles that many couples face. In other instances, you might feel defeated, because you've realized that there is still much work to be done to reach the level of intimacy in your marriage both you and your spouse desire.

With all these mixtures of thoughts and feelings, above all, we hope you will find encouragement on these pages. Be encouraged in knowing that you're taking action to make your marriage stronger. Be encouraged in knowing that your best days as a couple are still ahead of you! Like sex itself, this book is meant to be enjoyable! Let's get started.

BACK TO THE BASICS + WHAT GOD SAYS ABOUT SEX

HOW MEN AND WOMEN VIEW SEX DIFFERENTLY

Sex is a beautiful, pleasurable and vital part of marriage, but sadly, most married couples aren't too thrilled with their sex lives. There are many reasons for this, but one of the main reasons is a simple misunderstanding about how men and women view sex differently.

These differences don't hold true in every case, but they're accurate in most marriages. I hope these explanations create a deeper understanding and a more intimate connection in your marriage.

These differences don't make one spouse's way "right" and the other "wrong." Rather, these differences (like all differences in marriage) provide an opportunity for a husband and wife to work together with mutual respect and thoughtfulness to serve one another and reach a healthy solution together.

It all begins with understanding your differences. Regardless of whether or not this list below is 100% accurate for you, talk to your spouse about his or her needs, desires and apprehensions. Greater communication creates better sex (and improves the other aspects of your marriage too)!

In most (not all) marriages, men and women view sex differently in the following ways:

1. Men view sex as a form of stress relief while women tend to need stress relief BEFORE being in the mindset to make love.

As you can imagine, this subtle difference in thinking can create HUGE amounts of unnecessary frustration and miscommunication. If each spouse will adjust his or her expectations accordingly and talk through this difference, you might instantly improve your sex life. For more on this, check out our video series at BestSexLifeNow.com.

2. During sex, men tend to worry about their PERFORMANCE and women tend to worry about their APPEARANCE.

Even for couples who have been married for decades and are very comfortable with each other, there is still often an element of **insecurity** in the bedroom. It can be awkward to talk about this, so most couples avoid openly discussing it, but opening up about your apprehensions and insecurities can bond you together in a new way. Vulnerability paves the way to intimacy.

3. Men tend to THINK about sex much more often than women and women tend to think about all the other aspects of the relationship much more often than men.

The average man has a sexual thought every thirty-seconds. It's literally on our minds ALL the time. Women think about sex as well, but usually far less often. Women tend to think about other aspects of the relationship and are more in tune with the emotional connection, areas of potential disconnect, verbal communication and non-verbal communication in the marriage. She craves connection in all of these areas. She will feel most connected sexually when she feels a strong connection in these other areas of the marriage.

WHAT DOES THE BIBLE ACTUALLY SAY ABOUT SEX?

When people think of a timeless book that holds the keys to great sex, their first thought might be the *Kama Sutra*, but I'd argue a better choice would actually be the Bible. Perhaps it surprises you to think of the Bible as a practical manual for your sex life, but I'm convinced it's the most important resource at your disposal to help you have a healthy sex life (and every other part of your life as well). Here's why...

God created sex. He created love. He created life. He created you and He has a beautiful plan for your life. *Regardless of your faith (or lack of faith), I'd encourage you to explore God's plan for sex, because the world's plan for sex is to create a culture of heartbreak, to objectify women, to break up marriages, and to cause pain and regret.*

God's plan is much better.

Here are seven Bible verses with some steamy and surprising truths about SEX (in no particular order)...

"The husband should fulfill his wife's sexual needs, and the wife should fulfill her husband's needs. The wife gives authority over her body to her husband, and the husband gives authority over his body to his wife."
1 Corinthians 7:3-4

Both the husband and the wife should make sexual intimacy and fulfillment a high priority in the marriage and each spouse should put the other spouse's needs ahead of his or her own needs. This mutual selflessness is the key to a great sex life, but it's also the key to a great marriage outside the bedroom.

"Kiss me and kiss me again! Your love is sweeter than wine."
Song of Solomon 1:2

SOMEWHERE ALONG THE LINE, people started believing the myth that God doesn't like sex or He doesn't want us to enjoy sex. Nothing could be further from the truth! Sex is a powerful gift and when enjoyed within a committed marriage, it should be passionate and pleasurable. Just read the book of "Song of Solomon" in the Bible, which is essentially erotic love poetry. God wants us to have this kind of passionate, playful intimacy within marriage.

"Now the man and his wife were both naked, but they felt no shame."
Genesis 2:25

IN MANY WAYS, this is the theme verse for the entire book. The first picture of sex and marriage the Bible paints for us tells us that the couple was naked but felt no shame. This is a beautiful image of the vulnerability, trust, honesty, transparency and intimacy that should create a healthy foundation for every marriage. God wants a husband and wife to be "naked" physically, spiritually and emotionally with one another. When you have a "naked marriage" with no secrets and total vulnerability, you can experience perfect intimacy without shame or fear.

"Don't you realize that your bodies are actually parts of Christ?
Should a man take his body, which is part of Christ, and join it to a
prostitute? Never! And don't you realize that if a man joins himself to
a prostitute, he becomes one body with her? For the Scriptures say,
"The two are united into one." But the person who is joined to the
Lord is one spirit with him."
1 Corinthians 6:15-17

SEX ISN'T JUST a physical act; it's a sacred, spiritual act as well. When we reduce sex only to an act of physical pleasure, we're "using" our partner instead of truly loving him/her. We're also creating a bond with this person that goes far beyond the physical.

This is why there is so much pain, confusion and heartbreak involved in broken relationships with sexual partners that don't exist with other kinds of relationships. This is also one of the many reasons why casual sex and/or prostitution are ALWAYS a bad idea.

"Let your wife be a fountain of blessing for you. Rejoice in the wife of
your youth. She is a loving deer, a graceful doe. Let her breasts satisfy
you always. May you always be captivated by her love."
Proverbs 5:18-19

LIFELONG MONOGAMY within marriage is the best plan for sex. God wants your sex life to be AMAZING, but it needs to be amazing with the person you married. If you start looking outside the marriage, then everybody gets hurt. Think of sex like fire and marriage like a fireplace.

When fire remains in the fireplace it gives off light and warmth to the entire house, but when you take fire out of the fireplace and spread it around to other places, everyone gets burned!

"But I say, anyone who even looks at a woman with lust has already
committed adultery with her in his heart."
Matthew 5:28

JESUS RAISED the bar high when it came to God's standards for a "faithful marriage." He taught that monogamy isn't just physical; it needs to be mental as well. If our thought-life is X-rated, then it's going to have a negative impact on experiencing true intimacy in marriage. We need to be "mentally monogamous" to experience all God intends for sex and marriage.

"Run from sexual sin! No other sin so clearly affects the body as this
one does. For sexual immorality is a sin against your own body."
1 Corinthians 6:18

SEXUAL SIN IS in a category of its own because of the devastation it causes. Many have been taught that all "sin" (breaking God's laws) is in the same category, and while all sin hurts God and people, sexual sin is in a category by itself because of the powerful, negative consequences it creates for everyone involved.

The Bible says so much about sexual sin specifically to PROTECT us from the consequences. Never trade temporary pleasure for permanent regret!

Most of us have some kind of sexual "baggage" from our past. It may come in the form of choices we regret or brokenness over abuse we have experienced. In either case, God wants to bring you healing and peace. God loves you more than you can imagine. Allow His love and grace to fill the cracks in your broken heart.

These seven verses aren't all the Bible has to say about sex or marriage. The Bible is a timeless roadmap for all aspects of life and love. If you'll apply these seven scriptures to your marriage, you'll be off to a great start, but if you'll make the entire Bible the roadmap for your life, you'll always be headed in the right direction!

WHY SEX IS MORE IMPORTANT THAN YOU MIGHT THINK

So many times, I (Ashley) hear wives complaining about their husbands always wanting to have sex. Friends, I have been there too.

It's not that we don't enjoy sex or feel the need for it; it's just that our desire doesn't seem to be nearly as strong as our partner's. Please understand, wives can certainly have a stronger sex drive than their husbands, but in most cases, the husband has the stronger drive.

In either case, this can be a HUGE problem in a marriage when we refuse to talk about it. So, let's talk about it...cue *Salt-N-Pepa's* famous 90's song, "Let's Talk about Sex," in the background (just a little humor to loosen us up a little).

But, really, Friends, we need to talk about sex with our spouse. Sex is more important than you think, and you need to be having it more than you think. This is one of many important lessons I have learned in my own marriage.

When we got married, Dave and I had saved ourselves for each other. This wasn't easy, nor were we perfect in every way, but we made it to the wedding day without having sex.

I was so excited about the wedding night, but also extremely nervous, as you can imagine. Needless to say, it was great but it took some getting used to. I really liked it, but Dave LOVED it.

Ahem. I know this might feel as awkward to read as it is for me to write it right now, but I'm just being honest.

The more I have talked and counseled other married couples, the more I have found that this is pretty common. There is usually one spouse that has a greater need for sex. And, that's okay.

I didn't realize this truth as a newlywed, and it gave me a lot of anxiety. I started to think something was wrong with me. Why didn't I want to do it as much as Dave? How many times a week is normal? And, so on.

My anxiety certainly didn't help my desire, if you know what I mean. It was really awkward for a while, but then I read a book called *His Needs, Her Needs*, by Willard F. Harley, it all clicked for me.

Harley explained that in most marriages there is usually one partner who has a stronger need for sex and will want to have it more frequently. He also said that the couple should try to aim to have sex as frequently as possible to fulfill this need and protect the marriage. As we've pointed out throughout this book, the Bible has A LOT to say about sex too!

I love how *The Message* paraphrases 1 Corinthians 7:5,

> *"It's good for a man to have a wife, and for a woman to have a husband. Sexual drives are strong, but marriage is strong enough to contain them and provide for a balanced and fulfilling sexual life in a world of sexual disorder. The marriage bed must be a place of mutuality—the husband seeking to satisfy his wife, the wife seeking to satisfy her husband. Marriage is not a place to "stand up for your rights." Marriage is a decision to serve the other, whether in bed or out. Abstaining from sex is permissible for a period of time if you both agree to it, and if it's for the purposes of prayer and fasting—but only for such times. Then come back together again. Satan has an ingenious way of tempting us when we least expect it. I'm not, understand, commanding these periods of abstinence—only providing my best counsel if you should choose them."*

Did I mention how much I LOVE how the Message paraphrases

these verses? It's so good and so clear. Here are a few key points that stand out to me in these verses:

1. We should **NEVER** use sex as a *punishment* or *reward*.
2. We should **ALWAYS** seek to satisfy our spouse's sexual needs.
3. We should **ONLY** be engaging in sexual acts with each other and no outside source of any kind (i.e. porn or other people).
4. We should **RARELY** abstain from sex, but there are certainly times that it is permissible.
5. We must **ALWAYS** do our best to avoid sexual temptation outside the marriage and protect our marriage from sexual sin.

There is so much at stake, our marital intimacy, our sexual health, and most importantly, our commitment to the one we love most. We must strive to get this right.

God designed sex specifically for marriage. He wants us to have a healthy, enjoyable and thriving sex life with our spouse. Let's not withhold this act of love and service from each other!

4

HOW OFTEN SHOULD A MARRIED COUPLE MAKE LOVE?

In my years of working with married couples, I've discovered that many marital problems can be traced to issues, struggles and frustrations related to SEX. Most couples face the frustration of having one spouse with a consistently stronger sex drive than the other which often leads to question, how often should a married couple have sex?

Below, I've listed six reasons why more frequency in your lovemaking could help you, but before we get there, I want to do something different. Instead of launching into this discussion with stats and opinions, I'm going to do something unexpected. I'm going to share what the Bible has to say on the subject. You might have thought the Bible was boring or irrelevant, but it's actually the greatest marriage manual ever written! Here's one surprising passage about sex in marriage:

> *"The husband should fulfill his wife's sexual needs, and the wife*
> *should fulfill her husband's needs. The wife gives authority over her*
> *body to her husband, and the husband gives authority over his body to*
> *his wife. Do not deprive each other of sexual relations, unless you*
> *both agree to refrain from sexual intimacy for a limited time so you*

can give yourselves more completely to prayer. Afterward, you should
come together again so that Satan won't be able to tempt you because
of your lack of self-control."
1 Corinthians 7:3-5

This passage above is essentially saying that a married couple should make love as often as either one of the spouses wants to. This is pretty revolutionary. When a couple waits until both spouses are equally in the mood, it will rarely happen!

This model requires a mindset of mutual submission and selflessness for the sake of the other which will not only improve your sex life, but it's also a great approach to improving the other aspects of your marriage.

As it relates to your marriage, I'd encourage you to make love as often as the spouse with the higher drive wants to. This isn't practical 100% of time, but make it your goal not to "deprive each other" and as the frequency of your lovemaking increases, your overall connectedness as a couple will probably increase as well (for the reasons listed below).

When a couple isn't consistently connecting in the bedroom, it can start having some major repercussions in other areas of the relationship. When you make consistent lovemaking a habit in your marriage, you'll be strengthening the marriage in all kinds of ways. Here are just a few examples of how more sex in your marriage could have huge impacts:

1. It will bring you and your spouse closer together on a physical, emotional and even spiritual level.
2. May studies have suggested that high sexual frequency can impact your overall health and well-being.
3. A recent study on CNN.com suggests that frequent sex (they defined it as at least 3-4 times per week) could actually make you more successful and profitable in your career.
4. Greater frequency can lower levels of stress and sexual frustration in your marriage.

5. Greater frequency can statistically lower the risk and temptations that can lead to adultery.
6. Greater frequency is FUN. Do you really need more reasons?

WHAT EVERY MARRIED COUPLE NEEDS TO KNOW ABOUT SEX

Sex is one of the most powerful gifts God ever created. It was designed to bring a man and woman together in a physical, emotional and spiritual bond that would create pleasure, intimacy and also procreation. Marriages that neglect or misuse this gift are headed for frustration and maybe even divorce.

I was reminded of this when some friends of mine were having a marriage crisis and headed for divorce. They had drifted far apart and felt that there was no marriage left. As a last effort, they decided to take a *"30-Day Challenge"* and committed to having sex every day for a month.

By the end of the month, their marriage was stronger and their intimacy was reignited. Their marriage had new momentum, which has carried them forward. They're the first to say that *"it takes a lot more than sex to build a strong marriage, but it's nearly impossible to build a strong marriage without it!"*

Better sex in your marriage requires having the right mindset and establishing the right habits. These ten facts don't represent a comprehensive list, but this is a great start! If you'll apply these ten things in your marriage, I believe your sex life will instantly and dramatically improve!

Here's a quick "top ten" list of some of the vital facts every couple needs to know about sex (in no particular order).

1. You should probably be having more of it!

Healthy couples make sex a priority. I'm convinced that many (if not most) arguments in marriage stem from sexual frustration. When this aspect of the relationship is neglected, the marriage will start to deteriorate even when other areas of the marriage seem to be going strong. When you make love, you're making your marriage stronger.

2. Most men see sex as a form of stress relief, BUT most women need stress relief BEFORE they can be in the mindset to make love.

There are neurological reasons for these differences and this is also proof that God has a sense of humor! A husband and wife need to be in tune to each other's needs and desires and selflessly strive to serve each other. Men and women tend to be wired up differently and each person has his or her own wiring that often supersedes these broader generalizations. Get to know each other. Don't make assumptions. COMMUNICATE and your sex life will improve.

3. Remember that foreplay is an all-day event!

Foreplay doesn't begin five minutes before you're hoping to get it on. It should begin the moment you wake up in the morning. Every text message, every hug, every act of service, every phone call, every wink, every kiss, every "I love you," and every interaction with each other is an opportunity to make a connection that could culminate in a great climax for you both!

4. Men, if you want to get your wife in the mood, try "Chore-Play." Do the dishes or fold some laundry.

Most men are visual. Seeing their wife in lingerie is enough to instantly get in the mood. Most women are more complex in their process of becoming aroused. Sure, ladies want their man to look his best, but she also wants her mental to-do list to be clear so she can focus (like we addressed in #2).

Guys, you can help her get in the mindset by doing some household chores. You'll never look hotter in her eyes than when she catches you doing the dishes or folding some laundry!

5. Most people have some sexual "baggage" that they haven't fully discussed with their spouse. Bringing this out into the open could lead to a positive breakthrough in your sex life and in your marriage.

I've interacted with married couples for years, and I've found that there are a lot of sexual secrets spouses keep from each other. Some of these secrets are the result of past abuse and some are the result of past choices.

Some of these secrets can also stem from fantasies that one spouse is afraid to say out loud for fear of judgment or rejection. The bottom line is that you need to talk about all of these things with your spouse. *Secrecy is the enemy of intimacy.* If you want to grow closer to your spouse inside and outside the bedroom, bring your secrets out into the open and encourage him or her to do the same.

6. You should be physically monogamous AND mentally monogamous.

It's sad that we live in a world, where I have to clarify this, but monogamy is the only way a marriage can work. Don't look outside your marriage to fulfill your sexual needs, and I would argue that this includes porn.

Bringing another person into your bed or your mind will eventually destroy the intimacy. God intended sex to be enjoyed exclusively between a husband and wife. Your sex life starts with your thought life. Keep your thoughts and fantasies focused on your spouse.

7. Better sex starts with getting better in other areas outside the bedroom.

When communication is better, your sex life will usually improve, so talk, text and flirt with each other throughout the day. When you're serving each other's needs in other areas (*Guys, this means be willing to do the dishes and help more around the house*), your sex life will usually improve. When you show genuine thoughtfulness to one another throughout the day, the night is more likely to end well!

8. Don't use sex as leverage, a reward or a punishment.

In some marriages, sex (or denying sex) is used as a way to reward or to punish the other spouse. Over time, this practice will cheapen the power of sex, cause resentment and also erode the trust and intimacy in your marriage. Never use sex as a form of leverage, control, reward or punishment. See it as a sacred gift to be freely enjoyed together in marriage.

9. Don't put your sex life on hold while you're raising your kids or you might wind up with an "empty nest" and an "empty marriage"

When you're raising kids, it takes more time and intentionality to prioritize your sex life, but it's well worth the effort! In fact, I think one of the best gifts you can give your kids is the security that comes from seeing their mom and dad in a loving, affectionate, committed relationship with each other.

Obviously, still lock the door while the kids are in the house, but "grossing them out" by kissing and being affectionate with each other is actually a good thing. Have the kind of marriage that makes them actually want to get married someday!

10. Have fun!

Sex is supposed to be fun, so enjoy it! As you do, you'll find your stress levels decreasing, your laughter increasing, and a more positive outlook on life together.

6

LOVE IS NOT ENOUGH, AND HERE'S WHY

Love is not enough. It never will be.

The world defines love as a feeling and something we fall in and out of, which means we can lose the love that someone has already given us. This is especially disheartening when it comes to marriage. If love is just a fickle feeling, then how in the world can any of us stay married for life?

The truth is, we can't...if THAT'S what love is.

The good news is God doesn't define love this way. 1 Corinthians 13:4-8 says,

> *"Love is patient, love is kind. It does not envy, it does not boast, it is not proud. It does not dishonor others, it is not self-seeking, it is not easily angered, it keeps no record of wrongs. Love does not delight in evil but rejoices with the truth. It always protects, always trusts, always hopes, always perseveres. Love never fails. But where there are prophecies, they will cease; where there are tongues, they will be stilled; where there is knowledge, it will pass away."*

And, verse 13 goes on to say,

"And now these three remain: faith, hope and love. But the greatest of these is love."

Wow. THAT'S real love. That's the kind of love that I want to have for my husband, not some wishy-washy, tepid love. I want the kind of love that lasts forever.

When we are committed to someone or something, we offer that person or thing lots of time, attention and devotion. Sadly, there are many of us who are more committed to our hobbies and jobs than we are to our own families.

When we marry, we vow, or commit, to love our spouse for all the days of our lives. When we have kids, we are committed to raising our kids to the best of our ability and to never give up on them, no matter what.

In friendships, we are committed to being there for our friends in times of need and protecting their reputations. As Christians, we show our love and commitment to Christ by praying, reading the Word, and doing what He's called us to do the very best we can.

True love, God-designed love, requires commitment.

When life is hard and our relationship seems to be more difficult than usual, our feelings will change. But, our commitment can be unwavering when we CHOOSE to stay committed through thick and thin.

That is precisely why love, as the world knows it and defines it, is not enough. But, love, as God designed it and defines it, IS.

We can't choose our feelings. We're human. But, we can choose to love someone enough to be committed to him/her.

This is how marriage is supposed to work. When both partners choose to love each other by staying fully committed to one another on a daily basis, the marriage will thrive. Let's strive for THAT kind of love, Friends; a love and a commitment that will never fail.

TIPS TO SPICE UP YOUR SEX LIFE

7

THE EXCUSES COUPLES GIVE FOR THEIR BORING SEX LIVES

Recently, I (Ashley) was talking to a friend of mine about her marriage. She said that in almost every way, her marriage was better than ever–except when it came to the bedroom. When I asked her why she felt like things had fizzled, she said that they were both bored with their sex life.

And, they weren't on the same page when it came to their "sexpectations," and both of them had fallen into the trap of making excuses for their less-than-desirable sex life. Unfortunately, this couple is not alone in their predicament.

Here are four of the most common excuses married couples give for their boring sex life (and how to make it better).

1. "I don't have a strong *desire* for sex very often–if ever–anymore."

This is a common statement, however, most couples fail to find out the reason WHY a spouse is almost never in the mood. It could be a medical issue or an emotional/mental one. No matter the source, there are things couples can do to find out the root cause of the lack of desire.

They can go to their doctor and have some tests done to see if their hormone levels are off, and if they are, there are a lot of different ways that these imbalances can be treated. If it's not a medical issue, a couple might consider going to a Christian counselor to see if the lack of desire is due to a past hurt or mental hang-up.

Counselors are trained to identify the root causes of our struggles, and they can help us to form a healthier perspective of our marriage and ourselves when it comes to sex. If you or your spouse seems to almost never be in the mood for sex, consider seeing your doctor or local Christian counselor right away.

2. "We just don't have enough *time*."

We are all leading busy lives with a lot on our plates; however, this is not a reason to neglect our marriage, including our intimate time with our spouse. If we truly feel like we never have time to have sex with our spouse, then we are simply TOO BUSY.

Something has to give. We need to sit down with our spouse and see what we need to remove from our schedule to make room for sex. It's as simple as that, but it is easier said than done. Once we make room in our schedules, we need to follow through on our commitment and do our best to have sex with our spouse on a more regular basis.

When you both prioritize time to be intimate with one another, your relationship will thrive (and let's face it–you'll both feel amazing, too).

3. "I'm just not *attracted* to him/her anymore."

This is a heartbreaking excuse, and unfortunately, it's a pretty common one. But, this excuse doesn't just stem from a lacking physical attraction to one another; it has a lot to do with outside influences like pornography. We live in a world obsessed with perfection and hypersexual behaviors. And, the porn industry is at an all-time high.

It's more accessible than ever AND more acceptable than ever in society. But, it spoils and sometimes destroys the marital bed. Pornography and porn-like images train our mind to only desire what they have to offer. Then, we become disillusioned and disappointed with our normal-looking spouse and sex life.

Sex is about so much more than the physical, although physical attraction is certainly part of it. We should be intentional about taking care of our bodies by eating right, exercising, and getting adequate rest as much as we can, but it's even more important that we tend to our hearts and minds. The couples with the best sex lives aren't necessarily the most attractive couples; they are the most emotionally connected and committed couples who refuse to settle for a boring sex life.

4. "Sex feels like a *chore*."

I've heard many wives (and some husbands) say this over the years, and I may have said it a time or two myself, to be honest. But, Friends, we've got to change our perspective on this. Sex is not a chore; it is a beautiful, God-given way for a husband and wife to connect, and it should be extremely enjoyable too.

We can't allow exhaustion, kids, jobs, responsibilities, and anything else to rob us, our spouse, and our marriage of sex. We must stop seeing it as just another "thing" on our to-do list. At the same time, we must do our very best to make it a priority.

As a spouse, one of our responsibilities is to fulfill each other's sexual needs. But, approaching sex as a chore can be a major turn off to our partner. So, instead of viewing sex as some daunting task on our list, let's get excited about it.

Wear some lacy underwear, light a candle or two, send flirtatious texts throughout the day to one another, and get yourself in the mood for some intimate time with one another. Have fun with it, and make it your mission to truly make your spouse's day. Then, sex becomes something exciting to look forward to and something the two of you will enjoy together.

8

HOW TO GET YOUR WIFE "IN THE MOOD"

When I (Ashley) was young, there was a book called *Men are from Mars, Women are from Venus,* and it was flying off the shelves. As a kid, I thought this was a pretty cool title, but I had no idea what it meant.

Now that I have been married fifteen years, I get it. Husbands and wives aren't the same. Sometimes, it can even feel like we're from different planets, especially when it comes to what gets us in the mood for sex.

I want to address what generally gets women in the mood. And, it's probably a little different from what you are expecting, Husbands. Here are 4 ways to get your wife in the mood:

1. Open up to your wife through conversations.

When it comes to sex, a woman's emotional state directly affects her sex drive. We want to feel close to our husbands before we become intimate with them. So, we can't argue and hurt each other's feelings one minute only to flip a switch and hop in bed the next.

For most women, we need to verbally and emotionally make amends before any "make-up sex." And, it can't be flippant or forced,

Husbands. She needs you to hear what she's saying, AND she wants to hear your response, straight from your heart.

No nods or "uh-huhs". Tell her what's on your mind and heart. Don't hold back. She wants to connect with you through intimate conversation BEFORE physical intimacy. This is counter to how most men operate, but it is essential to keeping a thriving and mutually enjoyable sex life in our marriage.

2. Compliment her appearance and efforts often.

Recently, I met with a young wife and mom who was experiencing marital problems. Through our conversation, she mentioned that she often felt belittled by her husband because he would criticize most household tasks that she completed.

He would come home from work and immediately point out that the dishes were loaded incorrectly in the dishwasher and the towels weren't folded right, one thing after another. Over the years, this constant criticism has taken a great toll on their relationship, and it has made their sex life forced and not enjoyable.

Our words carry great weight with them, and criticism is toxic to our marriage. Husbands and wives can't compliment each other too much. Kind words to one another are vital to a thriving marriage.

Husbands, instead of dwelling on what your wife *should've done* or she's *doing wrong*, focus on all the things she's *doing right*. And, TELL HER about it, OFTEN. This will do wonders for your marriage and sex life.

3. Be affectionate with her, without expecting sex in return.

I know this can be very difficult for men because sex is at the forefront of their brains, but it is a must. Some women are more affectionate than others, but some non-sexual affection needs to happen BEFORE sex. Women generally aren't "hot and ready" like Little Caesar's pizzas or even "hot now" like Krispy Kreme donuts; we are more like sit-down dining establishments, we require a little more time.

When a husband rubs his wife's feet, holds her hand, massages her shoulders, etc., it helps to ease any tension she is feeling. And, it's also a nice, romantic gesture. It might even give you both a chance to connect more through a conversation that naturally ensues, and it will certainly show your wife that you love and adore her.

Even though it may lead to the bedroom, it's important that the husband does this without rushing through it or putting pressure on his wife to get to the bedroom. This is a time to slow down, look into each other's eyes and connect.

4. Take something off her to-do list.

As stated before, women view and think about sex differently than men. I've heard it said that if our minds were computers the men would only have one window open at a time, and the women would have multiple windows open all over the screen at one time. This resonated with me, and I think it is spot on.

Most women have a to-do list on their minds throughout the day. When a task is completed, we mentally close that window. If it's not finished, it stays open. Sadly, sex often becomes one of these windows. We want it, but it's hard for us to get in the mood with so many things to do.

As wives, we need to resist the temptation to make sex with our husbands just another "to-do" on our list. It's so much more than that, and it's so important to the health of our marriage. However, I do think husbands can certainly play a role in taking some things off of our list.

Wives always think their husbands are attractive, but we think he is smokin' hot in those rare moments when he is doing the dishes and folding laundry! When you are in the beautiful trenches of raising kids, the to-do list is astounding. And, it's awesome to have an active, helpful partner beside you, so you can navigate your long list of tasks together.

When we don't feel bogged down by our to-do list, our minds are freed up to think about awesome things like romance and intimacy. So, Husbands, please lend a hand, and know that you aren't just checking something off the list, you are romancing your wife with some amazing "chore-play."

9

SEXY WAYS TO GET YOUR HUSBAND'S ATTENTION

Wives, do you ever struggle to get your husband's attention? I think most of us have been there a time or two. As women, we want to know that our husband is attracted to us and desires us passionately. We want to feel that chemistry like we had at the beginning. Ladies, the spark is still there. We just need to get the fire going again.

When life gets hectic and the pressures of expectations and obligations set in, sex can just become another thing to "do". This is a sad reality that will hurt our marriage. If/when you find yourself in this dynamic, you've got to do something about it.

How can we get our husband's attention and get him in the mood? As wives, how can we spice things up and bring back the romance in our marriage?

Well, Girls, there are five (fun) and sexy ways to get your husband's attention.

1. Send flirtatious texts throughout the day.

Technology can hinder our marriage when we give it more attention than our spouse. Why not make technology work FOR us, not against us? Use it to spice things up a bit. Text your husband throughout the day. Tell him that he is on your mind and that you can't wait to see him later.

You can be as sexy as you want to with it, just keep in mind that your kiddos might pick up the phone and accidentally see those words or pictures later. Whatever you decide to send him, be sure to build anticipation for the romantic time you'd like to experience with him later in the day.

2. Give him a sexy greeting he will never forget.

This one requires a little planning, but it's a lot of fun. Plan to arrive home from work before your husband does one day. If you have kids, make sure they are safely occupied with a movie or board games. Before he gets home, put on your longest coat (with the most coverage) and shoes (as if you have been out and about or at work). What you wear underneath the jacket is up to you — be it sexy lingerie or your birthday suit.

When he gets home, you'll have a goofy grin on your face and a surprise in store that will certainly get his attention. If you have kids, be sure to guide him to the bedroom or another private area (with locked doors) before making the big reveal and having some "alone time."

3. Invest in some nice lingerie.

Men are extremely visual. Like many women, I like having something nice from Victoria's Secret every once in awhile, but I used to wonder why men like lingerie so much. Isn't the point for the garments to ultimately come off? I asked my husband about it one time, and he pretty much said lingerie is like sexy wrapping paper on your favorite gift.

Girls, I like my comfy cotton undies too, but I also know that they aren't nearly as appealing as a lacy bra and panties. And, you don't have to spend a fortune at Victoria's Secret. You can go to more affordable places like Target and Marshall's and get several sets! Your husband could care less where you buy the lingerie, but he will LOVE seeing you in it. And, who knows? It just might make you feel pretty sexy too.

4. Surprise him with an overnight date.

This one takes some creative planning if you have kids, but it is worth it. Tell your hubby that you are planning a surprise date night for the two of you. Arrange for a family member or a reliable babysitter to stay overnight with the kids. Go out to a nice dinner, a concert, a walk, a movie, or whatever you please.

Instead of going home at the end of the date, surprise him by driving to a nice, local hotel. Order room service, spend time in the hot tub (if available), go get a late night snack together, and of course, make love. He will LOVE it, and you will too!

5. Initiate when he least expects it.

Dave and I have met with numerous couples with marriages in crisis. Whenever the subject of sex comes up, the husbands are quick to say that they wish their wives initiated sex more. The wives almost always respond the same way, "I would if YOU ever gave me a chance!"

Girls, I get it. I do. Men usually have the stronger sex drive, but this doesn't mean that women don't want it too. Some of us don't think about sex nearly as often as our husbands do. We want to initiate, but they often beat us to it. Then, how do we initiate?

We do it when he least expects it. It's important to note that we can't just pick the most convenient time for us. We can't do it when we are bored because he's watching the game or tinkering in the garage. The goal is to catch him off guard and excited to engage.

Be creative. Here's one idea: call him up and ask to meet him for lunch at the house. Before you even get to the meal, initiate a quickie with him. He won't expect it, but he will think it is the best lunch break ever.

The longer we're married, the easier it is to fall into the "zombie marriage trap." Don't let this happen in your marriage. Put forth the effort. It definitely takes both of you, but someone has to make the first move. Try these five sexy ways to get his attention and spice up your marriage.

EMBRACING YOUR SEXINESS IN THE BEDROOM

Not too long ago some girlfriends and I started talking about our marriages over lunch. One of my friends shared that she feels like her husband is never satisfied with the frequency of their sex life, and she is frustrated because she feels insecure with her body.

"I mean, I've had a bunch of kids. I don't look anything like I did when we were first married. I just don't feel sexy."

The more we talked, the more the women in our group agreed that they also deal with a lot of insecurity with their bodies.

Can you relate? I certainly can. There have definitely been times when I've felt pudgy and unattractive, and sex was honestly the last thing on my brain. So, I get it. However, the truth is that the less often we have sex with our spouse, the less DESIRE we have for sex.

And, we fall into a terrible cycle of having little to no sex and both spouses find themselves extremely frustrated and even bitter toward one another. That's why it's important that we do our best to overcome these body issues and work to cultivate and maintain a great sex life with our husband.

Here are some practical ways to do that.

1. Choose to embrace your body as it is currently, and don't stress that you don't have your personal "ideal" body at the moment.

This can be hard, but it is a game-changer when it comes to enjoying sex. We can't fully engage in sex and be worrying about our stretch marks or cellulite at the same time. In fact, it totally stresses us out. According to a recent NBCNews.com article, stress kills a woman's libido.

Laura Berman, Ph.D., director of the Berman Center for women's sexual health in Chicago, says, *"Stress makes you tired, distracted and unmotivated to do anything, much less have sex. When a woman is stressed, the hormonal changes in her body trigger a chemical reaction causing sex hormone–binding globulin to bind with testosterone cells, so they're unavailable for libido and sexual response."*

In other words, the stress we feel when we think about our body not being what we think it should be ends up killing our desire for sex altogether. So we need to intentionally shift our thoughts.

The next time personal body-shaming thoughts start to fill our mind, we must SHUT IT DOWN and replace those with positive thoughts. For example, let's see our few extra pounds as curves instead of cellulite. Odds are your husband really loves those curves anyway. As women, we tend to hold ourselves to crazy standards based on air-brushed, photo-shopped models that don't even exist.

Ladies, let's stop torturing ourselves and embrace the body that we have NOW. Let's choose to love ourselves.

There is nothing sexier than confidence, and this confidence and intentional self-acceptance will also help us to destress and be more in the mood for romance.

2. Start having sex more frequently with your husband.

At a recent conference, a friend of ours shared that she had extreme anxiety about having sex with her husband after having their first child. She felt exhausted and totally insecure about her "mom-bod" to the point that she dreaded the day when the post-partum six-week waiting period was up and she and her husband could make love once again.

When the day arrived, her husband was patient with her, but she completely froze up and all she could do was cry. Weeks went by. A month passed and her husband patiently waited. She could feel a distance growing between them, even though her husband was being so understanding and tender with her. Eventually, she realized that she had to do something.

When she shared her predicament with a close friend, her friend looked in her eyes and plainly said, "You need to have sex with your husband today. Stop dreading this day and just go for it, or you'll just keep feeling anxious about it and frustrate him to no end."

My friend knew that this was the truth that she needed to hear and live out. So, she went to her husband, and they made love. Then, they did it the next day and the next. As my friend recalled this story, she said that something happened that she never expected. The more she and her husband made love, the more her desire for sex increased and her anxiety subsided.

Friends, sometimes we just need to go for it, regardless of our hang-ups. This doesn't mean that we discount our feelings or our husband's feelings.

Sometimes, we may be facing deeper issues that we need to address with a Christian counselor or doctor. Whatever the circumstance, we should be willing to do whatever it takes to get to the root of why we aren't having sex.

And, we should do our best to make sex a priority in our marriage. The more frequently we make love with our spouse, the more we will desire it and the less stressed we will be.

3. Invest in some sexy lingerie.

I used to think that lingerie was kind of ridiculous because the whole point of wearing it was for it to end up on the floor. Right? But, over the years, I've seen what a turn on it can be for both husbands and wives.

Most men love for their wives to wear lingerie because they see it as sexy gift-wrapping with all the lace and bows. And for most women, the very act of wearing lingerie can make them feel sexy and in the mood.

You don't have to spend a lot of money or get something uncomfortable. In fact, there are so many styles and sizes available these days. So give it try. Go shopping for a pretty bra and lacy panties, and surprise your husband with your findings when he gets home. You'll be surprised at how sexy you'll feel, and your husband will LOVE it!

Bottom line, we all have insecurities about our bodies, but we can choose whether we allow these insecurities to negatively impact our sex life and marriage. Ladies, let's choose to overcome.

Let's choose to see our bodies as beautiful and sexy just as they are. Let's choose to be confident and make sex a priority in our marriage. When we do this, we will enjoy a thriving sex life and a stronger, more connected marriage.

11

HOW TO BE AN "ATTRACTIVE" HUSBAND

Men, I'm going to let you in on a little secret: Your level of "attractiveness" to your wife doesn't have all that much to do with your physical appearance. Sure, she would appreciate it if you took care of yourself and made some effort to look (and smell) nice, but those are probably not the most important factors to her.

You don't have to look like one of the guys from Magic Mike or have six-pack abs to be the man of her dreams. You just need to do these five things to be incredibly attractive to your wife.

1. Take the time to be a good dad.

If you have children, taking the time to be an attentive and thoughtful father will do more to make you "attractive" in your wife's eyes than nearly anything else. You don't have to be a "perfect" dad (because there's no such thing), but you have to be present and you have to be consistent.

2. Help out around the house.

Statistics show that even in situations where both spouses work full-time outside the home, the wife usually still ends up doing the majority of the work around the house. Men, when we will roll up our sleeves to help around the house, your wife will take notice. Who knows where those chores might lead! Think of "Chore-Play" as a form of foreplay!

3. Continue to pursue her.

When you were first dating your wife, you were probably doing thoughtful and romantic gestures all the time, but as life goes on, the pursuit probably slowed down.

Your wife still wants and needs your continuous pursuit. She wants you to tell her she is beautiful. She longs for spontaneity and adventure with you. Find ways to keep showing your love, affection and pursuit of her heart in every season of your marriage.

4. Give her your best, not your leftovers.

As men, we can be tempted to give the best of ourselves to our careers or hobbies and then give what's left over to the people who matter most.

When you will choose to consistently give your best to your wife by investing time with her, listening to her, serving her, protecting her and encouraging her, you will be much more attractive in her eyes than you could imagine.

5. Be open and honest with her about everything.

She wants to know what you're thinking. She wants to engage with every part of your world, so let her in. She feels deeply connected to you and attracted to you when she knows she can trust you completely.

Don't hold anything back from her. Don't have secrets or passwords she doesn't know. Secrets sabotage marriages. The level of your trust and communication will ultimately determine the level of your marriage.

12

IS ANYTHING "OFF LIMITS" FOR A MARRIED COUPLE IN THE BEDROOM?

I (Dave) was recently having lunch with a friend and he shared some frustrations he was having in his sex life. I asked him if he wanted to elaborate (not because I was trying to pry into the intimate details of his marriage or be a creepy voyeur, but because both online and in person, I try to be a safe place for people to voice whatever struggles they might be having in marriage).

He immediately opened and said, "When we first got together, there were no limits in our sex life. My wife was ready to act out any fantasy I could imagine. Both of us had a wild past and our views of sex had been shaped by our own experiences and a lot of exposure to porn.

We even watched a lot of porn together as a way to spice things up in our own sex life. Our relationship wasn't great but our sex life was amazing. When we got serious about our faith, we realized that porn was 'out of bounds' in a Christian marriage.

Jesus taught that to look at another person with lust is to commit adultery in your heart. It was tough to give up, but we both felt like it was the right thing. The problem is that while now our marriage is better overall, our sex life feels like it's at an all-time low."

I asked him to elaborate and he said, "There are certain things that porn taught me are just part of sex, and they're things we used to do that she doesn't want to do anymore." I didn't ask him for specifics, but I was pretty sure he was talking about oral sex and/or anal sex, which are both acted out in pornography with as much frequency as vaginal intercourse. I know this from my own past struggles with pornography.

He said, "I feel like with her not being willing to do 'it' anymore, she's not wanting to give all of herself to me in the same way she used to and even in the same way she has given herself to many other men in her past. I mean, I'm her husband and she's giving me LESS than she gave to random men she hooked up with before we were together."

As my friend continued to process these complicated thoughts and feelings, I started to realize that his frustration with his sex life wasn't just the result of a physical act that was now not happening; it had an emotional aspect to it as well.

Sex is never just a physical act. He was picturing his wife giving "all of herself" to other men in her past in a way that she's not now willing to give to him. He was taking her preference to stop doing certain things as a slap in the face. It was like she was saying those other men in her past were more worthy of her uninhibited sexuality than he was. He wasn't just feeling sexually frustrated. He was feeling rejected and disconnected from his wife.

He asked with frustration in his voice, "Other than hurting each other or bringing someone else into the act (swinging), I don't think ANYTHING should be 'off limits' in the bedroom for a husband and a wife! Am I wrong?"

That's a great question, isn't it?

I told him that he needed to talk openly about these issues with his wife, and not just in a demanding way trying to coerce her into complying with his specific desires. I told him that by withholding certain sexual acts, his wife probably wasn't trying to deprive him or give less of herself to him but to actually give more of herself to him. He looked really confused by that so I elaborated further.

I said that his wife had probably come to associate certain sexual acts as part of her painful and promiscuous past full of brokenness and regret. For her, certain acts probably brought up baggage that she wants to let go.

The memories of her past made her feel dirty, unworthy and slutty. She had been forgiven of her past as she was now, as the Bible describes, a new creation in Christ. She wanted to give her best to her husband as a pure bride, but to her husband, he felt like he was getting a prude instead of a bride. If God really created sex and wanted it to be at its best within marriage, then why were they both so frustrated?

I didn't claim to have all the answers here, but I told my friend that this (like most issues in marriage) wasn't about who was "right" and who was "wrong." It would be about both partners communicating with transparency and vulnerability to express their feelings and strive to serve each other's needs with selflessness, thoughtfulness, mutual respect and love to find a solution that strengthens their marriage. If they both would approach the conversation not with demands but with a desire to truly understand each other, they'd be off to the right start.

Every couple has to deal with issues in the bedroom. Your sexual intimacy can and should be one of the most fulfilling and FUN aspects of your marriage, but it won't happen automatically.

Both you and your spouse have baggage, expectations, hang-ups, hurts and a myriad of other factors that need to be communicated for both of you to experience physical pleasure, emotional intimacy and the spiritual oneness that God intends to happen whenever a husband and wife make love.

We know these issues can be uncomfortable to talk about, but they're vitally important. As husband and wife, you should be able to talk about anything. Get naked (both physically and emotionally). Get vulnerable. It will do wonders for your marriage.

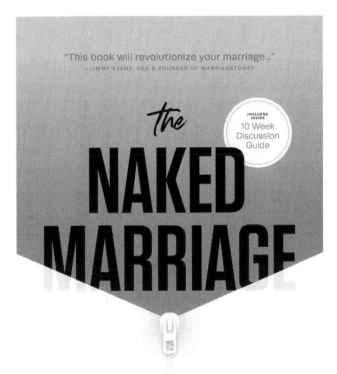

"This book will revolutionize your marriage..."
—JIMMY EVANS, CEO & FOUNDER OF MARRIAGETODAY

INCLUDED INSIDE
10 Week Discussion Guide

the

NAKED MARRIAGE

Undressing the truth about sex,
intimacy and lifelong love

DAVE & ASHLEY WILLIS
AUTHORS OF 7 DAYS TO A STRONGER MARRIAGE

The Naked Marriage

Also by Dave and Ashley
Imagine a marriage with amazing sex, but where great sex is only the
icing on the cake.

INFIDELITY + EMOTIONAL AFFAIRS

13

NINE RULES FOR PREVENTING INFIDELITY IN OUR OWN MARRIAGE

We've lived through the tragedy of seeing loved ones, respected leaders and close friends wreck their marriages through a single act of infidelity. Whenever we hear the tragically familiar story of another couple caught in the aftermath of a sexual or emotional affair, it's a wakeup call for us.

We want to do everything in our power to prevent infidelity, because we are convinced that without the proper safeguards, it could happen to anybody.

We know that our marriage, our family, our ministry and our credibility as advocates for stronger marriages could be instantly shot with one single act of infidelity. We refuse to allow that to happen, and we know we can't rely solely on willpower or good intentions to affair-proof our marriage and YOU shouldn't either!

Below are nine *Laws of Fidelity* we have adopted to safeguard our marriage. These might seem drastic to you, but I don't think there can be any lengths too great when it comes to protecting a marriage.

If you'll commit to these in your own marriage, you'll be safeguarding your marriage, your reputation and your legacy from the scars adultery can cause.

These nine "rules" are NOT motivated by a lack of trust in our marriage; they're motivated by a deep respect for each other and for the sacredness of marriage. I believe you can protect your marriage from infidelity if you'll do the following nine things.

1. Don't talk negatively about your spouse to others or online.

When people start venting about their husband or wife to friends or online, it's not just a harmless way to blow off steam and joke about frustrations. It's a dangerous opening that could pave the way for adultery.

The negative talk does several things: first, it chips away at the foundation of respect that must remain strong in every marriage; second, it sends the subtle message that you're not happy in your marriage and that you're "open" to someone who would treat you better. Be careful with your words. The tone of your words about your spouse will shape the tone of your marriage.

2. Never meet alone with a friend of the opposite sex.

We never meet up for coffee or lunch with anyone of the opposite sex unless it's a group setting. We work diligently to never be in public or in private alone with someone of the opposite sex.

This policy protects us from temptation, it honors our marriage and it protects our reputations from rumors. Even in one-on-one counseling situations with the opposite sex (which we try to avoid), we make sure to keep the door open. We don't want to create a scenario where whispers of improper conduct could even be entertained.

3. We see all of each other's text messages.

Our iPhones are set up with the same Apple ID where we both automatically receive each other's text messages. This keeps us in the loop of what's happening with each other. It's not motivated by distrust but by a desire to have total transparency and open communication in our marriage.

It's also a very practical safeguard against any form of inappropriate relationships forming. Being willing to share all of our texts also sends the clear message to each other and everyone else in our lives that we have a marriage with no secrets.

4. We share all our passwords.

This flows naturally from #2 about sharing text messages. We don't have a password or a PIN that the other spouse doesn't know. There are no hidden accounts, hidden emails, burner cell phones or anything else that would be off limits to each other. Other than a few surprise birthday parties and gifts, we have a "Secret Free Guarantee." In marriage, secrets are as dangerous as lies.

5. We don't watch porn or sexually explicit content.

Porn is an act of mental infidelity. I (Dave) will share my personal story (I used to be hooked on porn) in a later chapter. Even in R-rated movies or shows where there's a scene of gratuitous nudity or strong sexual content, we'll try to look away or skip the scene out of respect for each other. We want to remain constantly vigilant of the fact that infidelity never starts in a bedroom; it always starts in the mind.

6. We give "side hugs" to people of the opposite sex.

This might seem cheesy, but it's also very important. Some people hug members of the opposite sex with a full frontal assault that can border on an act of illegal groping. I never want physical touch to be misconstrued in any way, so even with close female friends, I try to stick with the side hug.

7. We don't engage in ongoing dialogues with people of the opposite sex on social media.

With the nature of what we do, we get hundreds of emails and Facebook messages per week. We do our best to respond, but whenever someone of the opposite sex seems to want to engage in an ongoing dialogue with either of us, we cut it off out of respect for each other.

Many affairs start by crossing lines on social media. You and your spouse may need to create a social media set of "rules" and boundaries to protect each other and your marriage.

8. We make time together a priority.

Affair-proofing your marriage isn't just about "defense" (eliminating unhealthy behaviors). It's also about being proactive when it comes to investing in your marriage. We are always looking for ways to spend time together, invest in our relationship and create resources to help other couples do the same.

Don't let your marriage get stuck on autopilot, or else there's a good chance it will crash someday! Keep investing into your relationship with each other!

9. We always wear our wedding rings.

A wedding ring is more than just jewelry. It's a daily reminder of the covenant you made to your spouse. It's a reminder that every choice you make will impact your husband or wife in some way, AND it's a symbol to the rest of the world that you are committed to your spouse. Certainly, people can cheat while wearing a wedding ring, but it's another line of defense against the temptation.

There are certainly other "rules" you could implement beyond these nine, and rules alone are never enough for a strong marriage, but if you'll implement these, you'll be doing a lot to protect your marriage. Some of these might seem countercultural or uncomfortable, but we're convinced that they're well worth the effort!

TO THE SPOUSE WITH A CLOSE FRIEND OF THE OPPOSITE SEX

It starts innocently. The two of you just connect. You have a lot in common and before you know it, you start looking forward to more encounters with your "friend". And that's all he or she is in your eyes... at least, for now.

That's what you tell yourself in your heart of hearts. You don't want to hurt your spouse, but this "friend" is such a good listener and makes you feel loved...desired...respected...wanted. Things you haven't felt with your spouse in a long time, but you've never really talked about it.

You start spending more and more time with this person and even go to lunch a few times. And, you tell yourself it's okay because, after all, you are JUST FRIENDS, right?

But, you find yourself sharing more personal stories than you intend to and locking eyes longer than you should. During your encounters, time tends to stand still, and every day you find yourself thinking about this person more and more.

Before you know it, you realize that some major boundaries have been crossed, and you are afraid to tell your spouse about it.

Does any of this sound familiar? If so, please know that you are not alone.

There's nothing wrong with finding a kindred spirit in another person. In fact, it's awesome–but, it's a slippery, nosedive of a slope when this close friendship is with someone of the opposite sex who is not your spouse. This may sound harsh and even ridiculous to you. I mean, we're all adults, right? We should be able to control ourselves and be "friends" with whoever we want…right?

Well, not exactly.

Would you be okay with your spouse having this same kind of "friendship"? Same conversations? Same encounters? Same attraction?

Probably not…right?

I know you love your spouse and would never hurt him/her on purpose. But please hear me–being close friends with someone of the opposite sex isn't good for your marriage AT ALL. As one who works with struggling married couples on a daily basis, it breaks my heart to see these "friendships" wounding marriages time and time again.

Close friendships with those of the opposite sex open up your heart and marriage to a world of hurt, and here's why:

1. Your frequent conversations with this friend are like cords of a rope–each one making the connection stronger and more intimate.
2. Your longing for more interactions is evidence of your desire to know this person more, and this is dangerous territory.
3. It is only natural for this connection to continue to progress to a physical, sexual relationship over time, unless you are intentional about putting boundaries in place and creating distance between you and your friend.
4. The excitement and allure of this new friendship is intoxicating and is harder to let go the longer it carries on.

I don't tell you all of this to make you feel bad; I tell you these truths to warn you and keep you from doing something that could devastate your marriage.

If you have a "friend" like this, then please do whatever it takes to put some distance between you. Create healthy boundaries and fight for your marriage. Go home and connect with your spouse—NOT this friend.

If you recognize that you are in pretty deep with this friend of the opposite sex and possibly have romantic feelings for him/her, then you need to confess this romantic affair to your spouse and seek Christian marriage counseling immediately.

This may be very difficult, and it will be hard for your spouse to process. But it's better to confess this now then to engage in a full blown sexual affair later. The two of you can get through this when you decide to fight for each other and do what is necessary to rebuild trust.

Don't let this opposite sex friend distract you from your commitment to your spouse. Your marriage is worth fighting for. Let this be a wake up call. It's not too late.

15

WARNING SIGNS OF AN EMOTIONAL AFFAIR

I recently received an email from a woman who was having an emotional affair.

The sad-but-familiar story began by describing a "friendship" she had developed with a man at work that eventually progressed into something much more. The relationship hadn't yet crossed into physical/sexual contact, but they were flirting with the idea and getting closer to those forbidden lines with each passing day.

She found herself in a confusing web of mixed feelings, and she knew this relationship now threatened to sabotage her marriage. She never thought she'd be in this position and that frustrated her. She'd been deceiving her husband and mentally planning out a new life with this other man.

She was asking herself, *"How did I let it go this far?"*

Even without crossing the line sexually, her situation is messy and will undoubtedly cause pain, but healing is possible. Still, these situations are much easier to prevent than they are to heal after the fact. That's why I often advise couples to be VERY careful about having close friends of the opposite sex, because most affairs start out as "friendships" that cross the line.

If you think that you (or your spouse) has let a friendship go too far, please take immediate action to create healthy boundaries and restore healing and trust in your marriage.

Here are the *7 warning signs of an emotional affair.* If ANY of these are happening with you OR with your spouse, please take immediate action before it's too late.

1. You're having conversations you hope your spouse doesn't find out about.

If you're ever in a position where you think, *"I'm glad my husband/wife isn't seeing this,"* then you're already out of bounds and you're playing with fire. A healthy marriage requires complete trust and transparency. Don't STOP flirting with your spouse and don't START flirting with anybody else.

2. You're dressing to impress a specific individual other than your spouse.

When we're trying to be visually attractive for an individual other than our spouse, we're opening a very dangerous door. Wanting to be professional and look your best is one thing, but wanting to look your best for one specific person is something else entirely.

3. You try to create opportunities to be alone with someone other than your spouse.

If you're going out of your way to "run into" someone so you can have one-on-one conversations, that's a huge red flag. You need to put immediate distance between you and him/her. Never trade temporary pleasure for permanent regret!

4. You delete texts or emails because you don't want your spouse to see them.

If you're ever hiding messages, texts or calls then you've crossed an obvious line and you're having an emotional affair. Secrecy is the enemy of intimacy in marriage. Confess to your spouse anything you've been hiding and start fighting to rebuild trust.

5. You are having romantic and/or sexual fantasies about someone other than your spouse.

Affairs don't start in the bedroom, they always start in the mind! If you allow your mind to play out fantasies, you're giving a piece of your heart to the object of that fantasy and you're opening the door for the fantasy to become a reality.

6. You're constantly comparing your spouse to another individual.

When you become emotionally involved with someone, the mental tendency is to see this new person as nearly flawless and, by comparison, your spouse's flaws become much more obvious. If you're more critical of your spouse while mentally comparing them to this other person, you're falling into a toxic trap.

7. You are dreaming about or actually planning a new life with this other person.

Once you start planning and romanticizing a new life with this other person, you're in a very dangerous place. I urge you to rethink what you're doing and confess to your spouse.

FIGHT FOR YOUR MARRIAGE! If any of these warning signs are happening with you or with your spouse, please take immediate action. MarriageToday.com has a great resource library for you.

16

SECRETS ARE THE ENEMY OF INTIMACY

A good friend of mine recently confided in me (Dave) that he cheated on his wife a few years ago. He's been carrying guilt and shame over the affair everyday since the one-night stand with a co-worker, but he said that he's decided not to confess this to his wife because it would only hurt her. In his mind, he has justified his secrecy as a way to protect his wife and his marriage.

We have worked with married couples from all over the world, and we've found that my friend's decision to keep big secrets from his spouse is a commonly held mindset. We live in an era where people value personal privacy over total transparency in marriage, and this secretive mindset is having some massive repercussions in the long-term health of our relationships.

Below I'm going to list out the six reasons I gave my friend why confessing the whole truth to his wife is far better than living with this secret. I hope this list prompts you to have the courage to pursue greater transparency and trust in your own marriage.

If you're currently dealing with a crisis or breach of trust in your own marriage, I'd also encourage you to check out MarriageToday's website for comprehensive online programs for couples in crisis.

1. Just like the title of this book, a marriage must be "naked" which means no secrets and total transparency.

When God created the first married couple, the Bible tells us that they were "...naked and without shame" (Genesis 2). That's really the theme of this entire book. Nakedness is a beautiful picture of what marriage really means, and I'm not just talking about sex here (although that's very important too).

A truly "Naked Marriage" means having nothing to hide from each other. It means full transparency. It means giving your spouse and all-access key to your heart, your mind, your hopes, your fears and every other part of your life. If you want to experience love and intimacy without limits, get naked (which also means getting honest).

2. Secrets create invisible landmines in your marriage that will explode in unintended ways.

When we carry around secrets of any kind, those secrets will not stay fully buried. They leave a residue on our attitudes and behaviors; they tend to expose themselves in unlikely ways. Most of our secrets will come out eventually and then we have to deal with the added aftermath of the secret itself plus the additional breach of trust that came with each day we chose to keep hiding it.

I dealt with this in my own marriage when I tried to hide an ongoing struggle with pornography. The porn itself hurt my wife, but the choice to hide it, instead of confessing it, hurt her as well.

3. Confession shows courage and character. Secrets show deception and dishonesty.

We want to hide our mistakes, sins and flaws from our spouse (and everyone else), but when we try to keep something hidden, it numbs our own conscience in the process. Secrets don't make us stronger; they make us weaker (and they weaken our marriages as well). If you made a bad choice in the past, please don't cover it up by making a bad choice every single day to deliberately and dishonestly hide it. No matter what it might cost you, the truth is always worth telling.

4. In marriage, any form of secrecy is really an act of infidelity.

In marriage, secrets are just as dangerous as outright lies. Every day you choose to keep something hidden from your spouse, you're essentially committing a form of infidelity ("infidelity" really just means "broken trust"). When we value our own privacy at the expense of the sacred vows we made to our spouse, we're chipping away at the foundation of trust that every strong marriage must be built upon. The moment you send a text message or visit a website you hope your spouse doesn't find out about, you're already in very dangerous territory.

5. A painful truth is always better than a hidden lie.

It hurts to confess a painful secret and it hurts to hear one, but it hurts far worse to carry the weight of a secret sin. Whenever we let something live in the dark, it controls us, but once we bring it out into the light, it can't control us any longer. Have the courage to confess.

6. Your marriage WILL get stronger when you both stop hiding things from each other.

When we keep secrets in an attempt to protect the marriage, we're actually weakening the marriage. We're building the relationship on a false foundation. If you really want your marriage to get stronger, take the *"Secret-Free Guarantee."* Stop hiding things. Bring it all out into the open. It might be a painful process, but it could take your relationship to a new level of health, wholeness and happiness.

PORNOGRAPHY

17

TO THE HUSBAND WHO LOOKS AT PORN (A WIFE'S PERSPECTIVE)

Every week, I (Ashley) receive numerous messages from wives who have discovered that their husbands are looking at porn, and it's heart-breaking. Porn can wreck a marriage. I know this pain, because I, too, have walked through it in my own marriage.

Early in our marriage, I logged into our computer and discovered that Dave had been looking at porn. I couldn't believe what I saw.

My heart was beating out of my chest, and I seriously thought that somebody had broken into our home and surfed the web for porn. Not Dave. Not my Dave. We had a great marriage–at least I thought we did.

All I could think was,

How could he do this to me? To us?
  Am I not enough for him? Am I not pretty/skinny/sexy enough?
  Doesn't he know this is wrong?
  Didn't he know this would hurt me?

I took an hour or so to process what I eventually realized and accepted as the truth: Dave had been looking at porn for a while. He had a porn addiction. My Dave. My husband. My hero.

I knew I had to address it. I called him at work and simply asked if he had something to tell me. He immediately confessed to the porn. It was like he'd been waiting for me to find out. He told me that he was glad it was out in the open now, and that he knew it was wrong.

I would love to tell you that the days that followed were easy, but they weren't. I was so hurt. I felt ugly and unwanted. I could tell that Dave felt horrible about it. He wanted to stop doing this a long time ago, but he said he just couldn't stop through his own willpower.

As a Christian, he understood that he was lusting after the women in those images. He knew what Jesus stated so clearly in the Bible, that to lust at a woman is committing adultery in your heart. It goes directly against our marriage vows.

Husbands, I share this with you, not to point fingers or to make you feel bad. I share this because I want you to know what your porn habit does to your wife.

It breaks her heart. It makes her feel like you cheated on her. It makes her doubt her beauty and sexual appeal. It causes her to have a deep insecurity with your marriage. It causes her anxiety and even depression.

It makes her feel cheap, and she sees you as sleazy. It fractures the trust she has in you, and it immediately makes her lose respect for you.

You may tell yourself the lies that so many other husbands in our culture believe. Lies like;

I'm not hurting anyone.

   I'm not actually sleeping with another person, so it's not cheating.

   What's wrong with me spicing up my sex life?

   This is something I do alone, so it doesn't affect her.

   Porn actually enhances my sex life, because it gives me ideas for what we can do in the bedroom.

   I'm a grown man, and I can do whatever I want to do. It's none of her business.

   It's okay if I look at porn to meet my needs, because she doesn't want to have sex as frequently as I do.

All of these are excuses that mask a HUGE problem and keep husbands intertwined in a terrible habit that can become a full-blown addiction.

Husbands, if you are looking at porn, please get help and STOP immediately. Go confess this to you wife. Don't hide it any more. Seek God's forgiveness and your wife's forgiveness.

Then, take the steps necessary to regain her trust. Put accountability in place. Remove computers or other devices from hidden places. Get blockage software that will alarm a trusted friend or your wife any time you look up porn on your computer.

Get rid of any television channels that show porn at night. Be willing to do whatever it takes to beat this and save your marriage. You can do this if you are willing to put in the work.

You must show your wife that you only have eyes for her. Show her that you want her and love her with all your heart. Give her your time and attention daily.

Those porn stars can't love you back. Don't trade the love of your life for a temporary, empty fix. Go to your wife and talk about your sexual desires and needs. Listen when she shares hers as well.

Work together on having a God-honoring and sexually satisfying marriage. Don't settle for a counterfeit image to fulfill a need that only your wife should meet.

Porn is never the answer. It doesn't spice things up. It chokes out real intimacy between a husband and wife. Please know that there is hope.

Dave and I grew stronger through this struggle, and you can too! If porn is a struggle in your marriage please get help. Our friends at XXXchurch.com have some resources that could help you get started.

18

THE TRUTH ABOUT WOMEN
AND PORN

Let's face it. We are all visual creatures, and nudity draws us in like flies to a bright light. This really isn't a bad thing. In fact, God made human beings this way on purpose. He made us sexual so that we can experience intimate pleasure with our spouse and possibly have children one day.

We are supposed to appreciate the naked body. We are wired to desire sex. It isn't gross; it's beautiful. Unfortunately, our culture often represents it as everything but the amazing gift that it is.

I (Ashley) recently watched part of an episode of a reality show that follows the glamorous lives of several famous married women. You might know what show I'm referring to, and it can be addicting to watch. During this particular show, one housewife was discussing what she described as the secret to her seventeen-year marriage.

She said that they both "worked at it" and did things to "spice things up" including watching porn together on a regular basis. She then commented that most of her friends didn't watch porn with their spouses, and she thinks that everyone would have better marriages if they watched it together.

I honestly couldn't believe how comfortable she was in admitting that this was a regular practice in her marriage. Even if it were true, most people wouldn't admit it on national television. She was not only admitting it; she was celebrating it and even advising it. I couldn't help but ask myself, "Is porn really becoming this socially acceptable?"

Here are four surprising and startling facts about women's use of pornography.

1. More women are consuming porn.

The more I've thought about this, I've realized that this famous housewife's view of porn might be more common than I think. She's willing to call porn what it is in front of millions of people, instead of giving it another name or denying her use of it all together.

The porn industry is a multi-billion dollar business that is growing everyday. It draws in more profits than all the television networks COMBINED. So, yeah, lots of people are watching it; and it's not just men. Statistics show that more and more women are paying for porn as well.

Although many will not admit to it, statistics show that most people have seen at least one explicit sexual act, willingly or otherwise, in their lifetime. Porn has certainly permeated our society, but it's not just through the porn industry itself, even though the profits are astonishingly high.

Unless you are living completely off the grid, you may have heard of a little book called *Fifty Shades of Grey* and the two movies that have come out about it. I'll be honest; I have never read *Fifty Shades* but I have talked with many friends that have.

I've also seen the movie trailer, and well, it's racy to say the least. Please don't misunderstand me. If you are not a Christian, I don't see any reason why you didn't pick up the book. Who wouldn't want to read about an extremely good-looking, successful and mysterious man who supposedly sweeps a young, innocent and sexually inexperienced young lady right off her feet?

Did I mention that it has been described as "graphic" and a "guilty pleasure"? I get it. I do. No wonder more than 100 million copies have been sold worldwide, according to the *New York Times*.

For those of us who are Christians, I think we have to pause here and ask ourselves how God wants us to respond to all of this. Again, I am speaking to myself here. *Fifty Shades* isn't the first salacious novel and movie to pop up in our culture, and it won't be the last.

When we read novels filled with erotic scenes, our brains respond in a very similar way as if we are watching an explicit sexual act. For many women, it is all about the fantasy. That is the very reason many of us end up reading these novels. What we fail to realize is that we are opening ourselves up to lustful thinking that doesn't involve our spouse, and this is detrimental to our marriages. In

Matthew 5:28, Jesus gives us a sober warning against lust when he tells us,

> "But I tell you that anyone who looks at a woman lustfully has already committed adultery with her in his heart."

The same goes for women looking at men lustfully.

2. Many women believe porn is harmless (but it's NOT).

We tell ourselves it is harmless because we aren't engaging in the act, but Jesus clearly raises the standard for Christians here and states that thinking about it is just as sinful as doing it. He doesn't tell us this to be a huge buzz-kill or to make life extra hard; he is trying to teach us how to guard our mind and hearts against sexual sin.

As Christian wives, we are called to only have eyes and longings for our husbands. Allowing ourselves to be gripped by the lustful thoughts that are sure to come from these seemingly harmless, sexually-driven novels or movies only train our minds and hearts to be unsatisfied with our own sex lives.

It's so easy to compromise our beliefs when it comes to this. I, too, have read a little too much, looked a little too long, and pondered longer than I should have. That is exactly what lust does to us. It seems so innocent at the time, but it is an act of subtle disobedience that only leads us down a road of insecurity and emptiness, not to mention broken relationships.

3. Porn decreases actual intimacy with your spouse.

Throughout our marriage ministry, my husband, Dave, and I have talked to many couples contemplating divorce. When we would try and get to the root of their marital issues, they would often share that they had not had sex for months or even years.

In many of these situations, the husband was frequently looking at porn and the wife was filling the void with novels, movies, and nights out with girlfriends. They had lost interest in each other, and they considered themselves to be "out of love".

What they failed to see was the common denominator: lust. They had stopped desiring each other, so they were seeking to fill their sexual desires elsewhere. Sometimes, these husbands and wives would end up having full-blown emotional or physical affairs, which only made the road to healing much more difficult.

4. There is hope even if you feel addicted to porn.

I am not sharing all of this to make anyone feel guilty or hopeless because I know otherwise. God loves us and understands us. He will forgive the repentant. There is hope. I have seen husbands with a hidden porn addiction find the road to healing and restore their marriages.

I know wives who have turned away from a lifestyle filled with lust and loveless marriages only to find that they can have a completely fulfilling marriage on all levels with God's blessing. We don't have to accept whatever our culture deems as socially acceptable.

If we want our marriages to be strong, we must turn our hearts and minds to God and he will help us to keep our eyes, minds, and hearts from wandering. He will bless all aspects of our marriages, including the sexual. You don't need porn or some made-up steamy novel to spice up your marriage anyway.

So, let's keep movie characters, empty novel fantasies, and ridiculous porn scenarios out of our bedrooms and enjoy the beautiful intimate union that we can have with our spouse.

19

MY PAST STRUGGLES WITH PORN

What I (Dave) am about to share is very uncomfortable to talk about, but I'm stepping way outside my comfort zone to do it so that I can help as many people and strengthen as many marriages as possible.

I've read that as many as 95% of all teens will view explicit pornography (either accidentally or on purpose) at least once before they graduate from high school. I fit into those statistics.

As a teenager, I looked at porn and felt guilty about it. I'd go through a vicious cycle of secretly looking at it and then feeling guilty and hating myself and staying away by sheer will power for as long as I could but then returning to it again.

This continued through college. Sometimes there were long stints in between my "relapses" which gave me the false sense of security in believing I had overcome it, but I learned over and over again that I had not overcome it.

Eventually, I bought into the myth that once I got married, it would cure itself, because having a beautiful wife (which I do) would automatically remove the temptation of wanting to look at anyone else, but the secret and shameful cycle continued even after I married the love of my life the week after graduating college.

She found the evidence on our home computer and she was heartbroken. I had shattered her trust and I felt hopelessly ashamed.

As painful as it was to have my secret out in the open, it was what had to happen to start the healing process. I only wish I would have had the courage to confess before getting caught. Regardless, getting caught was a gift from God because once the lies are dragged out into the light, even though it hurts at first, it's the first step towards healing.

That was a decade ago, and thankfully, God and my wife both showed me a lot of grace, which has helped me break free. It took trusting God and putting safeguards and accountabilities in place to retrain my thinking, and today, I'm so thankful to be living without that secret shame and constant temptation eating away at me.

Porn is having a HUGE impact on people and specifically on marriages. Some people view it as pure evil while others view it as harmless entertainment and even a helpful aid in "spicing up" things in their sex life. I definitely don't claim be an expert, but I want to briefly share my own story and a few insights that I've learned along the way.

Below are four of the most damaging lies about porn that I believed. These lies continue to seduce many people and damage many marriages. The more we view porn, the more we believe these lies and sabotage our relationships and ourselves.

Lie #1: Porn doesn't hurt anybody.

The truth is that it will hurt you and also harm your present and future relationships. In the Bible, Jesus said, *"To look at a woman lustfully is to commit adultery with her in your heart"* (Matthew 5:28), so porn, by its very nature, is an act of infidelity.

Lie #2: Porn is harmless fantasy.

The truth is that this type of "fantasy" is a direct enemy of true intimacy. It programs your mind to think of sex as just an animalistic act with many partners and no emotional attachments. It's an enemy of intimacy.

Lie #3: Porn is so addictive that I will never be free of it.

The truth is that you can be set free, but you have to rely on God's power instead of your own will power. If you're reading this and you're currently struggling, you are not alone! The first step is to admit that it's wrong and that you want to make it right. You can overcome this, but don't try to do it alone. Confess it to your spouse and to God. Ask forgiveness. Put safeguards in place. There are some great resources to help get you started at **XXXchurch.com.**

Lie #4: Being in a healthy marriage to an attractive spouse will remove the temptation.

Porn doesn't train you to be satisfied by a healthy relationship; it warps your mind to never be satisfied.

DON'T LET porn lie to you anymore. If you'll do those things, you will discover the life-changing promise of Romans 12:2 which says,

"Don't copy the thinking of this world but be transformed by the renewing of your mind, then you'll discover God's will for you which is good and pleasing and perfect."

HANGUPS AND ROADBLOCKS TO GREAT SEX

20

"CHRISTIAN" SEXUAL BAGGAGE

Sex is a beautiful gift from God. I (Ashley) think we can all agree on this. However, many parents and churches treat it like the "secret we should never speak of." So, we inadvertently leave it to the world, and it is speaking loud and clear.

But, we can't blame the world for over-sexing our kids when we've practically taken ourselves out of the driver's seat and handed the world the keys. From the Internet, to the salacious magazine covers in grocery aisles, to sexy television commercials, social media, "reality" TV and easy access porn, sex is everywhere! As Christians, ones who love and know the Creator of ALL things-including sex, we must take it back and teach our children the truth.

As a teen, I was part of an amazing youth group that discussed all of the "hot topics" of the day. They would even have question-and-answer sessions in our small groups. So, when sex happened to be the topic, many of us were eager to hear what our leaders had to say.

One of my friends nervously raised her hand and asked the leader, "Um...how far is 'too far' when it comes to making out?" The leader paused for a moment and then proceeded to tell us, in Christian code language, that she was basically one kiss away from an orgasm, so it was probably wise to not even kiss a boy until you are married. As you can imagine, I left that small group conversation very confused and kind of grossed out. I couldn't believe that *kissing* was considered off limits too.

You see, for years I had learned that sex was a huge, shameful no-no, and I would nearly ruin my life if I ever even thought about doing it. I know my parents and church had good intentions in teaching me this way, but to be honest, it just made me scared of sex.

I think this is how many parents and churches roll. We don't want our kids to be doing it, and rightly so, but we don't want to open the door and have a real, honest conversation about how good sex is either.

I think that some of us are afraid that if kids know that sex is a "good" thing, then they will have a higher likelihood of having pre-marital sex. These kinds of conversations also force parents and church leaders to think about our own past sexual mistakes, and we aren't comfortable talking about this with our children. We are afraid that our kids will think things like:

- *Well, Mom and Dad didn't wait, so why should I?*
- *Dad had multiple sexual partners before he met Mom, and everything turned out okay for them. So, I'm not waiting."*
- *My leader got pregnant in high school, and she has a wonderful life today. So, having sex before you are married really isn't a big deal.*

I get it. Sometimes, it's hard to know how to properly address sex without revealing some holes in our own stories. None of us are perfect. We all make mistakes. But, we can't let this keep us from having honest, age-appropriate discussions about what the Bible says about sex, and it says a lot!

The Bible is crystal clear that Biblical knowledge and wisdom should be our compass and foundation for the full life that God wants for all of us. I think most Christian parents and churches would say that they are doing the best they can to teach the Word to their kids, and yet, many of us fall short when it comes to sex. But, sex is an important part of life. When we don't address it head on, we are basically allowing the "world" to explain it to our kids. 1 Corinthians 3:19-20 gives us a sober warning when it says,

"For the wisdom of this world is folly with God. For it is written, 'He catches the wise in their craftiness', and again, 'The Lord knows the thoughts of the wise, that they are futile.'"

As parents and church leaders, it is our heart and purpose to train our children up in the way they should go, and sex must be a clear part of this "training." We can't shy away from it no matter how awkward we think it may be. Proverbs 4:10-12 says,

"Hear, my son, and accept my words, that the years of your life may be many. I have taught you the way of wisdom; I have led you in the paths of uprightness. When you walk, your step will not be hampered, and if you run, you will not stumble."

This is how we must approach teaching our kids about sex. We must explain the clear boundaries that need to be in place, teach the truth about how God designed sex, and delineate how to make wise choices in this over-sexed world.

So, what does the Bible really have to say about sex?

1. It is a **BINDING** covenant that is physical, emotional, and spiritual. (Genesis 2:24)

2. Sex is designed for a **HUSBAND AND WIFE** within their own marriage. (Genesis 1:27 and Hebrews 13:4)

3. It is **GOOD**. (Genesis 1:31)

4. Sex is meant for **PROCREATION AND PLEASURE**. (Genesis 1:28, Proverbs 5:18-19, 1 Corinthians 7:3, and Song of Solomon 7:1-3 and 6)

These are all POSITIVE things about sex within the union of marriage. They aren't something to be scared of at all. Each of these point back to the fact that sex is truly a gift from God, not a curse. As parents and church leaders, we need to be taking more of this positive angle when teaching our youth about sex.

This doesn't mean that we don't explain the natural consequences that come from having sex outside of God's boundaries. Kids need to realize that being careless with sex opens us up to the shame that comes with sin.

We give a part of ourselves away to someone we haven't committed to in the eyes of God. We use people for pleasure. We place our feelings and desires before our fundamentals and dedications. When we choose to have sex outside of God's boundaries, we are settling for less than His best for us.

Our kids need to know these consequences, but these should NOT be the first things our kids understand about sex. How can our children understand the negative consequences of careless sex unless we teach them God's broader, beautiful and good plan for sex first?

This is where I found myself so lost as a young girl. With good intentions and in an effort to keep me chaste, my parents and youth leaders primarily taught me about the life-altering consequences of careless sex instead of how sex masterfully fits into God's plan for marriage and family and that it is a GOOD thing.

So, I pushed my feelings down deep and prayed for God to help me to save myself for marriage. And, I did, with God's help. I couldn't wait for my wedding night, but I was honestly scared to death. The only thing I knew about the actual act of sex was what I learned in health class and what I saw on television; so, not much.

Dave and I had a wonderful wedding night, but it took me a long time to overcome the belief that sex is a shameful, hurtful and dreadful act. I had a hard time "flipping the switch" from a young, willfully chaste woman to a married woman who could fully embrace the beautiful gift of sex with my husband.

I'd been bound and determined to not do "it" at all costs for all of my youth, and then–*boom*– I could be uninhibited. It was difficult for me to reconcile this in my mind and heart, and it took some time for me to shake this negative programming. And, I've found this to be a similar hurdle for many other Christian youth who were taught to fear sex.

Friends, we must STOP doing this to our youth, because it sets them up for confusion and disappointment once they are married. As Christians, we should have the BEST, most-fulfilling sex lives around because we are sons and daughters of the One who designed it and His Word defines it.

Let's bring God's truth about sex to light and stop letting the world set the standards of sex for our children. We can do this, but we MUST be willing to start and continue the conversation.

21

HOW AND WHEN TO TALK TO YOUR KIDS ABOUT SEX

Not long ago, my seven-year-old son picked up a Maxim Magazine at the barbershop and his eyes quickly bulged out of his head as he flipped through the pages filled with bikini-clad young ladies. Ashley quickly noticed and put the magazine back telling him it's not polite to stare at ladies' bodies.

A few minutes went by and she noticed he was staring at a "Field and Stream" magazine with the same intensity he'd had with the Maxim, so she investigated and found that he had snuck the Maxim inside the Field and Stream.

He was busted, and his little face turned red. He shook his head and said, "I'm sorry, Mommy, but I really like looking at those ladies!"

A few weeks later, during bath time, he said, "Dad, today on the playground, one of the kids was talking about S-E-X."

I didn't know if he knew it was a real word called "sex" or if he only knew of it by it's three infamous letters (like the CIA or FBI). I smiled and calmly asked, "S-E-X, huh? What do you think that means?"

He thought for a moment and said, "My friend said it means when two people are boyfriend and girlfriend."

In just a minute, I'll tell you what I told my seven-year-old about

S-E-X, plus an age-specific chart of what to say and when, but first, I'd like to address a few important points about how (and when) to start having "The Talk" with your children.

I recently read a very insightful book called *Touchy Subjects: Talking to Your Kids About Sex in a Touchscreen World*, by David Dean and my friend, Craig Gross, who is also the founder of XXXchurch.com and iParent.tv. Some of the insights below are straight from this book, and I'd encourage you to read it if you have young kids or adolescents.

In no particular order, here are some things to keep in mind when communicating to your kids about sex and other "touchy" issues.

1. They're hearing about it much earlier than you'd think.

The Internet has opened up a new world to this generation of kids, and consequently, they're hearing about sex younger than any previous generation. According to XXXchurch.com, the average age of first exposure to pornography is now ten-years-old. That means the typical eleven-year-old has seen explicit porn before she has ever had a conversation about sex with her parents.

2. They are getting mixed messages.

It should come as no surprise that the mixed messages about sex on the school playgrounds, Internet, Netflix and other easily accessible sources are going to leave kids confused. That means we, as parents, need to be starting these age-appropriate conversations early and keep the dialogue going consistently through every season of their development.

3. They want to be able to talk about anything with you.

It might seem super awkward, but believe it or not, your kids crave the kind of relationship with you where they can talk about anything. Don't hide from touchy subjects. You don't need to have the "perfect" thing to say. Kids aren't looking for perfection; they're looking for your availability and authenticity.

Practically, here are some age breakdowns that seem to work:

- **Ages 7-9:** Introduce the subject. Ask what they've heard. Start the conversation.
- **Ages 9-11:** Begin to talk about the biological and moral aspects of sex in an age-appropriate way. A great tool to help with this is "Passport2Purity" from FamilyLife.com. It created some very healthy and helpful conversations with my ten-year-old son and I plan to use this same resource with all our children.
- **Ages 11-13:** Address the physical changes they're experiencing and share stories from your own questions and experiences when you were going through those same changes.
- **Ages 13+:** Keep your thumb on the pulse of what's happening with their peer group, recognizing that with each passing year, more of their friends will become sexually active. Reaffirm your values often, but also bring up the subject without a judgmental tone to keep the dialogue open and transparent. Talk about gender identity and other issues they're being confronted with. "Passport2Identity" from FamilyLife.com is a great resource for this age group.

So, back to my seven-year-old son's question about S-E-X, here's what I said:

"Buddy, I'm so glad you feel comfortable talking to me about this. I always want you to be able to talk with me about anything. You're going to be hearing a lot about sex from your friends and maybe on TV, and most of what you'll hear won't be true.

As you get older, I will explain more about this, but for right now, the main things you need to know are that sex is a beautiful gift God made for a Mommy and a Daddy who are married and it's part of His perfect plan for making babies.

It's beautiful, but it's also private, so just like you don't talk about your private parts or other people's private parts on the playground, you shouldn't be talking about sex either. If you ever have any questions about sex, or about anything, else, I want you to always feel comfortable asking me, okay? I love you, buddy."

I'M sure I could have said some things differently or better, but he seemed to respond well. I'm still trying to figure out this whole parenting thing! Thankfully, God gives a lot of grace for the journey.

FALSE BELIEFS THAT WILL HURT YOUR MARRIAGE

Mark Twain once said,

> "It's not the things you don't know that will hurt you; it's the things you know for sure that just ain't so!"

When it comes to modern marriages, I can see a lot of truth's in Twain's wit and wisdom. Some of the marriage assumptions we have been taught to *"know for sure"* simply aren't the truth. When we operate under false assumptions, we are setting ourselves up for failure. I hope that clarifying some of these common "marriage myths" below will help us all refocus our relationships towards healthier and happier homes.

Ten common *"marriage myths"* (in no particular order):

1. If I married the "right person," I should always feel in love.

Our culture has fed us the myth that we all have a perfect "soulmate" out there and if we find him/her, our passionate feelings will never fade, our disagreements will be rare or nonexistent, we'll both want to make love with each other constantly and every day in marriage will have fairy tale bliss.

When we wake up one morning and don't have those feelings, we start to assume we must have married the wrong person and need to get out and find our real "soulmate." The truth is that strong marriages are built on commitment not compatibility.

2. If my spouse really loves me, he or she will be willing to change.

Some of the most frustrated people on earth are the ones who are in a marriage where they're trying to "change" their spouse—or they're in a marriage where their spouse is trying to change them! It's exhausting and unnatural. It reduces the marriage to manipulation instead of love.

Yes, both spouses will certainly have to make selfless adjustments for the marriage to thrive—but neither should do it at the expense of losing his or her identity in the process. Love brings out the best in us, but it doesn't change who we are. Remember, it's never your job to "fix" or to "change" your spouse. It's your job to love your spouse. Love is what truly changes us all.

3. My friends know me, so they're always the best place to get my marriage advice.

Nearly everyone in your life is going to offer you advice and share their opinions with you. We trust our friends, so we naturally assume their marriage advice is going to be solid, but the best advice is usually going to come from outside your peer group because your peers are dealing with the same stuff you're dealing with.

You need a mentor, not just a friend. You need to find advice and wisdom from someone who is ahead of you and probably older than you. Find someone with the kind of marriage you hope to have twenty years from now and ask them for advice.

4. Just because I'm married doesn't mean I can't keep secrets and have personal privacy.

This one always tends to offend people, but it's vital to a healthy marriage. Secrecy is the enemy of intimacy and if you want a healthy marriage, you have to have total transparency and trust.

This means don't keep secrets, hidden passwords, hidden money, hidden conversations or anything else your spouse doesn't have full access to. The healthiest couples value transparency over privacy. They place their responsibility to their spouse ahead of their rights to privacy.

5. My parents raised me, so my loyalty to them should be stronger than my loyalty to my spouse.

We should always honor our parents, but when we do it at the expense of our marriage, we've created a toxic and dysfunctional dynamic. Your first loyalty must always be to your spouse. Practically speaking, this means you shouldn't talk disrespectfully about your spouse and you shouldn't allow anyone in your family to talk disrespectfully about him or her either.

6. I shouldn't have to tell my spouse what's wrong. If he or she was paying attention, they should know!

One of the most common miscommunication traps in marriage happens with these unspoken assumptions. We think our nonverbal hints should be more than enough to get the message across—or we think the answer is so obvious that we shouldn't have to say it out loud. When we fall into this trap, one spouse stays clueless and the other spouse stays frustrated. We need to communicate with consistency, clarity and transparency.

7. As long as I don't commit adultery, I should be able to do anything I want to get my sexual needs met.

Modern couples have adopted the destructive habit of "outsourcing" the sexual fulfillment in their marriage to outside sources like pornography or romance novels. In an attempt to enhance their own sexual gratification, they're actually sabotaging the sexual intimacy of their marriage.

When you replace your spouse with another person (virtually or physically), then you're pursuing pleasure at the expense of your marriage. All your sexual energies, fantasies and desires should be focused on your spouse. Monogamy should be both physical and mental. It might sound impossible, but it's not.

8. Every couple is unique, so there's not a single "right" way to be married.

This one is partially true, but it's often the "almost true" things that prove to be more deceptive than obvious lies. Every couple is unique and there's no cookie-cutter approach to marriage, but there are some timeless and universally applicable principles that provide a compass to keep a marriage on course.

To disregard these principles and write our own rules for love and marriage will lead to disaster. I outline the timeless principles that should be present in every healthy marriage in my book *The Seven Laws of Love: Essential Principles for Building Stronger Relationships.*

9. Our kids need us, so they should always come before our marriage.

If you're a parent, I'm sure you'd be willing to give your life for your kids. Parenthood takes that kind of selfless concern for our kids, but I've seen too many couples be "marriage martyrs" by sacrificing their marriage on the altar of parenthood.

The parents wrongly assume that total devotion to the kids requires putting the marriage on autopilot. Those parents wake up one day to realize they have an "empty nest" and an empty marriage!

One of the greatest gifts you can give your children is the security that comes from seeing their parents in a loving, committed marriage. Have the kind of marriage that makes your kids actually want to get married someday!

10. If things aren't working out in the marriage, I would probably be better off with somebody else.

When you face struggles, don't look for an exit strategy. Don't fantasize about a life with someone else. Work through your challenges together and you'll come out stronger on the other side. Remember that a "perfect marriage" is just two imperfect people who refuse to give up on each other!

23

THE SEX-KILLERS IN MARRIAGE

I've interacted with thousands of married couples (both online and in person) and I've discovered an alarming trend along the way: many (if not most) married couples are discouraged by the state of their sex lives. Many of these couples aren't sure why their sex life is so disappointing, so they have no idea where to start to correct the problem.

Married couples shouldn't live in a perpetual state of sexual dysfunction and disappointment. I know the reasons that cause sexual tension can be very complex, but I'm convinced that the most common twelve reasons are the ones below.

Every couple faces unique challenges, so not all of these will apply to your situation, BUT I hope this list helps spark some healthy dialogue in your marriage.

I also hope you'll commit to working together to improve the sexual intimacy and satisfaction in your relationship. It takes more than sex to build a strong marriage, but it's nearly impossible to build a strong marriage without it!

I believe these twelve factors are the primary "Sex-Killers" in marriage. If you tackle these issues, you'll make a tremendous difference in your marriage.

1. Feelings of inadequacy.

We're bombarded by airbrushed images of physical "perfection" and they can lead to unrealistic expectations and feelings of inadequacy. If you've fallen victim to this, please talk about it with your spouse.

Build each other's confidence. We've found that MOST women have some insecurities related to their appearance which hinders their sex life AND most men have insecurities related to their performance. In short, women need to hear, *"You're so beautiful"* and men need to often hear *"You're the man!"*

2. Hormonal imbalance.

Sometimes, a lack of sex drive or satisfaction can be attributed to an imbalance of your hormones. If you think this might be an issue for you, ask your doctor. There are some very effective treatment options that will not only help with sex, but will also help you feel much better overall.

3. Lack of communication.

I'm amazed at how many couples simply don't talk about the sexual aspect of their marriage. Talk about it. Share your fears, your fantasies and your frustrations. Better communication OUTSIDE of the bedroom will create better intimacy inside the bedroom.

4. Secrecy.

Secrecy is an enemy of intimacy. Sometimes a lack of connection sexually is a symptom of a deeper trust issue in the marriage. Secrets, lies and distrust of any kind in marriage will create a climate of insecurity, and will kill the intimacy in your relationship.

5. Poor physical health.

If you face a disease or injury that hinders your sex life, look for other ways to cultivate intimacy. In most cases, the physical limitations aren't the result of an injury or illness, but they're the result of neglect and poor habits that can and should be changed.

If you're out of shape, you're probably not going to have a vibrant sex life. Strive to make physical health (eating right, working out, etc.) a priority in your marriage. It will lead to more happiness and satisfaction both in and out of the bedroom.

6. Mental infidelity.

This one is going to step on some toes, but true intimacy in marriage requires not only physical monogamy, but also mental monogamy. Porn and racy romance novels have rewired our brains to live in a fantasy world that doesn't involve our spouses. Masturbation also falls into this category and, particularly for men who frequently masturbate, their sex life in marriage almost always suffers, because they're spending their sexual energy apart from their wife.

7. Resentment.

If there's a lack of forgiveness in your marriage, it will create a toxic force that will harm your sex life and most every other part of your relationship. If your marriage is suffering from a climate of disrespect, distrust or dysfunction, you need to take action to heal the marriage. The poor sex life is one symptom of a much larger issue.

8. Past physical, emotional or sexual abuse.

Tragically, many people have experienced some form of sexual abuse in their past. Abuse can cause deep and lasting scars. If the pain of abuse haunts you, I encourage you to seek out counseling. Not just for the sake of your sex life and your marriage, but for your peace of mind and emotional healing.

9. Sex as a bargaining chip.

Whenever you take on the mindset that sex can be given as a REWARD or withheld as a PUNISHMENT in your marriage, it cheapens sex and eventually causes resentment. When sex is seen as a transactional relationship (I'll do this for you if you'll do something for me), then your treating your spouse like a prostitute.

10. Exhaustion.

For those of you who have young kids at home or crazy work hours, you know how exhaustion can take a toll on the libido.

11. Consistent rejection from one of the spouses.

If one spouse is always the one initiating sex and the other spouse consistently rejects those advances, it will slowly kill the trust, the intimacy and the sex in the relationship. If you "have a headache" every night, you might need to just take some Aspirin and still make love.

See sex not only as a way to connect but also as a way to meet each other's needs. You are the ONLY legitimate way your spouse's sexual needs can be met. When you consistently deny him/her, you do harm on an emotional, a relational and a physical level.

12. You fill in the blank.

No two relationships are exactly the same, so your main issue may be nowhere on this list. Whatever your struggle may be, talk about it with your spouse. Work together to find a solution. Your marriage is always worth fighting for!

24

CANDID ANSWERS TO THE BIGGEST SEX QUESTIONS

As we approach the end of this book, we wanted to have one chapter dedicated specifically to giving specific answers to the most common questions we've heard about sex. We've received thousands of sex-related questions and these are answers to nine of the most common questions we've received about sex.

Many of these questions have been addressed in other places throughout this book, but we thought it would be helpful to have these questions and answers collected in one place to make them easier to access.

1. What's "okay" and what (if anything) should be "off limits" in the bedroom?

The *Fifty Shades of Grey* phenomenon has fueled a lot of questions about what's healthy and what (if anything) should be off limits. There is certainly a lot of freedom and creativity two spouses should enjoy in the bedroom but things that are destructive and harmful include:

Anything that makes one or both spouse's uncomfortable, anything physically dangerous to one or both spouses, and bringing another person into the bedroom (virtually or physically).

Healthy sexual intimacy is built on a foundation of monogamy and mutual respect. With that being said, we also believe that God intends sex to be FUN and adventurous within the covenant of a committed marriage.

Don't feel like you can't try new things together. If sex isn't fun and exciting, then you're doing something wrong! With that being said, don't try to coerce or pressure your spouse into performing acts he or she isn't comfortable doing.

2. Is pornography okay to use if we watch it together?

There's a lot of debate about this, but based on what the Bible teaches about lust and the statistics related to the destructive ramifications of porn, there's no place for porn in your marriage. Jesus said that to look at someone lustfully is to commit adultery in your heart. It's an act of mental infidelity.

Porn, even when watched together with your spouse, brings other people into the marriage bed and into your minds. It might feel like it spices things up in the moment, but the long-term impacts will be negative.

Porn desensitizes us from experiencing true intimacy. It reduces sexual intimacy as an act and it replaces love with lust. Lust looks at others as objects to be used for our own pleasure; love looks at others as souls to be cherished. Don't let lust creep into your marriage.

Keep your eyes and your thoughts focused on each other. Don't just be physically monogamous; be mentally monogamous too! It will make a big difference in your marriage.

3. Is masturbation okay?

Masturbation during intercourse with your spouse can be just a fun part of foreplay or reaching orgasm if your spouse finishes before you do, but what I'm talking about here is solo masturbation apart from making love to your spouse.

I used to have a struggle with pornography, and even after I broke free from porn, it took me several years longer to stop the habit of masturbating. I justified it in my mind and told myself it wasn't a big deal, but it was. My own thought life and sex life with my wife are better because I stopped masturbating.

I'd caution you against masturbating for several reasons. First off, it trains you mind to see sex as a selfish act, so even when you are making love to your spouse, your brain is just trying to get to the pleasure of your own orgasm instead of focusing on your spouse.

Secondly, it tends to conjure up images of lust, which are dangerous for reasons addressed in the above question about porn. Lust is the enemy of love. Finally, especially for men, masturbation will lower your drive and your performance when it's time to make love to your wife. You're giving your best energies to an act that doesn't even include her and then you won't be at your best for her.

4. My husband (or wife) has a much higher sex drive than me. What should I do?

It's common for one spouse to have more drive than the other. This issue, like most issues in marriage, can be improved through communication and both spouses being willing to work together to serve each other's needs. There could also be medical and/or hormonal issues that could be addressed with your doctor. Sometimes the solution is as simple as a hormone treatment or more physical exercise to increase health and libido.

There are other times when there's still a huge divide between one spouse's sex drive and the other's. In these situations, look for ways to serve each other's needs. Don't put your spouse in the position of living with constant sexual frustration.

It will eventually harm the marriage. You might say, "But I don't feel like doing it." If we only do the things we feel like doing, not much would get done. In fact, we'd probably all be divorced, because there will always be moments when we don't "feel" like being married.

Sometimes, giving your spouse a "quickie" might make a huge difference to them and it doesn't require a huge amount of effort on your part. I'm not saying one spouse should be able to use the other as an on-demand sex doll or anything like that.

What I am saying is that a healthy marriage requires two people that are so focused on serving each other's needs that everyone's needs are being met in the process. You might also find that the more you do it, the more you'll actually start wanting to do it!

5. I'm having a difficult time reaching orgasm. What should I do?

Women typically require more time and more stimulation to reach an orgasm. This means the husband needs to slow down, give more attention to foreplay and/or other stimulation and make it a priority for both spouses to climax. This, like all parts of marriage, benefits from honest communication. Tell your spouse what you like. Tell him or her what feels good.

Tell them if it's too fast or too slow. Don't expect your spouse to be a mind reader and don't apologize for being wired up differently than he or she is. Talk about these things during sex, but also be intentional about talking through these issues when you're not actually in the act of making love and communication is easier.

6. I feel like we're not connecting inside or outside the bedroom, and I'm not sure why. Any suggestions?

There can be many factors (physical, hormonal, emotional, etc.) that lead to a lack of "connection" in the bedroom. One of the most dangerous causes is secrecy. Anything you don't communicate to your spouse (or your spouse doesn't communicate to you) creates an invisible barrier inhibiting intimacy in your marriage.

Like we've discussed throughout this entire book, strive to have a "Naked Marriage" which means don't just be physically naked; be emotionally and spiritually naked. Don't keep secrets. Live with total transparency, vulnerability and honesty in your marriage.

It might seem a little scary to be that "naked" but it's the only way to experience real intimacy. Don't settle for anything less! It won't just improve your sex life; it will improve every other aspect of your marriage too.

7. Past hurts are causing complications in the marriage. Any suggestions?

Most people enter into marriage with some level of regret over past sexual choices or perhaps even wounds from past sexual abuse. There are also hang-ups that can be caused by broken trust within the marriage and a difficult time reestablishing trust and intimacy.

These are complex issues, but the first step is to commit to healing. If you've been wounded, take time to heal. You may need to pursue professional counseling. If there have been wounds in your marriage, forgive each other and work together to reestablish trust. Get to the root of the issue and then tenaciously work together to resolve it.

8. How often should a healthy married couple make love?

The preferred statistical average is a couple times per week, but this is really an issue to work out in your marriage. I'd suggest talking about it and leaning towards the preference of whichever spouse desires it more often.

It takes a lot more than sex to build a strong marriage, but it's nearly impossible to build a strong marriage without it! Make it a priority. It will make a big difference in your marriage.

9. How (and when) should I talk to my kids about sex?

We live in a world where kids are exposed to sexually explicit material and conversations at an earlier age than ever before. Your child probably already knows much more than you think he or she knows.

Don't look at a conversation about sex as one dramatic and awkward conversation. Look at it as an ongoing dialogue where you keep sharing age-appropriate information and building trust with your child so he or she knows they can talk to you about anything.

As far as covering all the specific details, don't think you have to fly solo. There are some great resources out there. I'd encourage you to look up the "Passport2Purity" resources from FamilyLife.com. That resource helped me tremendously in having those conversations with our oldest son and I plan to use them with our other kids as well.

25

ENJOYING SEX WHEN YOU DON'T LIKE YOUR BODY

One of the most common questions we receive from our blog readers reveals a growing trend in insecurities related to body image and how those insecurities negatively impact a married couple's sex life. We frequently get messages like this...

I want to be at my best for my husband/wife, but I'm so uncomfortable with my own body. I don't even want him/her looking at me because I feel gross.

I feel fat. I have stretch marks. I feel unattractive. I can't compete with the images of 'perfect' people I see all around me.

My insecurities are creating sexual frustration and friction in our marriage. What do I do?

We ALL have some level of insecurity. Even those "picture perfect" models often struggle with body issues. Being in perfect physical shape isn't the solution (although better overall health can be a positive factor), the real issues are deeper than the surface.

If you want to improve your sex life, but you and/or your spouse have insecurities or body image issues, please consider these three simple principles.

1. Remember what it actually means to have a "naked and unashamed" marriage.

Our first picture of the first married couple in the Bible's Book of Genesis tells us that Adam and Eve were "naked and unashamed." I'm sure they were in good shape, but they weren't "naked and perfect."

There were no other humans around to compare themselves to. It wasn't about comparison. It wasn't about looking in the mirror (because mirrors didn't exist).

They had a beautiful connection and intimacy because they were focused on each other's souls, not each other's physical imperfections. Find the courage and vulnerability to be "naked and unashamed." It will take time, but it will create such comfort, security and intimacy in your marriage bed (and every other part of your marriage too).

2. If you're uncomfortable making love with the lights on, try candlelight.

I know you might feel uncomfortable being seen, but your spouse wants to see you while you're making love. Especially for men, most guys are wired up to be more engaged and connected to their wife through visual stimulus.

You might not want to see yourself, but he wants to see you! If having all the lights on seems too intimidating, start with candlelight. The soft light is flattering to the figure and it also sets a romantic tone that could make you both feel more comfortable.

3. Remember that confidence is sexy (and confidence is a choice, not a feeling).

When we have physical insecurities it starts a domino effect. You don't feel sexy, so you don't want to think about sex, so you get uncomfortable when your spouse initiates sex, so your spouse gets hurt feelings and the marriage gets stuck in a negative cycle of perpetual frustration and miscommunication. If this is accurately describing the current dynamics in your marriage then you need to rewire your thinking.

Confidence is not just a feeling. You might not feel confident about yourself right now, but you can choose to project confidence and before long, you'll actually start feeling it. I'm not making this up!

There's plenty of research out there to back this up. Like the best-selling book and TED talk "Presence" point out, even your posture can make you feel more like a superhero and take your mind off your own insecurities. There's nothing sexier than confidence.

There are, of course, many other ways to improve beyond the three I listed here, but these three will give you a great start. Above everything else, remember to communicate to your spouse about everything. Better sex starts with better communication, and you'll discover that communication will also help you improve on the other aspects of your marriage as well.

CONCLUSION

26

HOW TO HAVE A HAPPY SPOUSE

When I was engaged and just a few days away from the wedding, my wise Dad said, "Son, always invest the best of yourself into your marriage. Put your wife ahead of yourself. Strive to make her a happy woman. A happy wife creates a happy life."

My parents have a wonderful marriage. They're best friends. They love each other AND they actually like each other too! They have the kind of marriage that made me genuinely excited about getting married someday, so I took dad's advice to heart. I've found it to be completely true! When my wife Ashley is happy, I'm happy.

Now, you might be asking, "How can I *make* my wife happy?" That's a great question, and a complicated one, because I don't think it's possible for one person to "make" another person happy.

In fact, when we expect a spouse to make us happy, both spouses usually end up unhappy. A lot of marriages struggle because both spouses are unhappy and blame each other for their unhappiness. Still, I've learned that there are some very specific ways a husband can and should cultivate happiness and joy for his wife.

I'm convinced that if you'll do this one thing, it will create more happiness for your wife and more peace and joy in your marriage. I've found we all tend to learn best through stories, so I'm going to illustrate this one principle through a true story that just happened in our marriage.

Ashley and I recently had the opportunity to take on a project that would instantly bring a good amount of additional income. I wanted to do it! I was already mentally spending the extra money. The problem is that the stress and strain of this project was going to fall mostly on Ashley.

She's already working so hard in so many areas and she doesn't have much extra margin to take on new projects. Still, she saw that I was excited about the opportunity, so to be supportive and encouraging to me, she agreed to do it. She's always so willing to support me (even when my ideas are bad)!

As we started making preparations to begin the project, I sensed the stress she was feeling. She insisted that she was fine and willing to take on the extra workload, but I knew she didn't have peace about it. I made the decision to pull the plug.

I knew that no amount of extra money would be worth taking joy or peace away from her. I told her that I didn't want to do it, because I'd much rather have the extra peace and joy in our home than the extra money and stress.

I could see the weight of that stress lift off her shoulders and then she gave me that smile that still melts my heart every time!

Honestly, it was a no-brainer! That little bit of extra money wouldn't have meant much when I'm at the end of my life looking back, but there's no price tag I could ever place on our relationship. Giving up this money was a small (but also a tangible) way that I could show her the place of priority she will always have in my heart.

So, what's that "one thing" a husband should do to make his wife happy (and vice versa)? It goes back to what my dad said to me all those years ago. It's simply to prioritize your wife's needs ahead of your own agenda. It's to show her that you value your marriage more than your money. It's showing her that her happiness is the key to your own happiness. It's showing her that she matters to you more than anything or anyone else.

I can't "make" my wife happy, but I've learned that I can fuel

Ashley's happiness when she knows that I value HER above any other relationship, pursuit or agenda. When she knows that she doesn't have to compete with my career, my hobbies or anything else to have the best of my time and attention, it gives her confidence and joy.

When she knows that I'm willing to sacrifice my own "agenda" for the good of our marriage, she feels protected and cherished. She deserves my best, not my leftovers. When I'm willing to give my best, she's much happier...and so am I.

27

WAYS TO "RECHARGE" YOUR MARRIAGE DAILY

One of the most frustrating things on earth is when you reach into your pocket to pull out your smart phone and realize it's completely out of power. You remember that you didn't charge it up, and now, it's dead.

You won't be able to play Candy Crush or check Facebook or text anybody until you find a way to recharge it. When something is important to us, we need to make sure it stays charged up.

Think about this simple concept in terms of your marriage. If your marriage is important to you, shouldn't you be intentional about "recharging" it daily? Shouldn't you make sure you're doing everything in your power to keep your relationship with your husband or wife powered up at all times?

Most of us would say we want a fully charged marriage, but we don't always know how to do it. There's not a simple instruction manual or a plug attached to your spouse that you could just connect into an outlet.

No, recharging a marriage requires much more effort than recharging a phone. Luckily, it's not as difficult as you may think. Below are ten ways to recharge your marriage daily (in no particular order).

1. Give a foot rub.

This might not sound glamorous, but it's very helpful. When you're touching your spouse (and not just sexual touch), it connects you on a physical and emotional level. Your conversations become deeper when you're touching while you talk. Plus, your spouse will really appreciate the massage!

2. Go to bed at the same time.

This one isn't always practical, but do it as much as you can. "Pillow Talk" makes for some of a couple's most intimate conversations, plus there's a lot more than talking you can do together in the bedroom!

3. Outlaw criticism.

I'm convinced that criticism (which can sometimes manifest itself in sarcasm) is one of the leading causes of marriage breakdowns. Your words have power to build up or to tear down. Your spouse needs you to be his or her biggest encourager; not their biggest critic!

4. Digital detox.

As much as you can, turn off your phones when you're around each other. Also, have some time together daily (even if it's only fifteen minutes or so) with no TV or distractions of any kind. Just talk. Enjoy each other free from all the noise of the outside world.

5. Flirt throughout the day.

Foreplay is an all-day event! Every chance you get, give your spouse a call or send a flirtatious text message. Let them know they're on your mind all day.

6. Find some good "couple friends."

Don't just have "his friends" and "her friends." Find some couples that have healthy marriages, strong values and fun personalities and enjoy time together with them. We end up becoming like the people we hang around the most.

7. Listen (don't just pretend to be listening).

Most of us are pretty good at giving the minimum amount of focus required to make our spouse think we're really listening. Instead, give your spouse your full, focused attention. We communicate our love by our listening even more than we do by our words.

8. Pray.

This one might freak some of you out, but I believe prayer is one of the most intimate acts a couple can share. End your day by holding hands and thanking God for each other (out loud) and asking Him to guide your steps. A marriage built on a foundation of faith is a strong marriage.

9. Laugh.

Laughter should be the soundtrack of your life. Never laugh at each other, but always laugh with each other! Don't take yourself too seriously or your marriage too lightly.

10. Learn.

Never think you've got it all figured out. Keep discovering new things about each other. Keep learning and growing together.

28

WAYS TO SAY, "I LOVE YOU" WITH YOUR ACTIONS

Love is the most important part of life. We all tend to agree on that, but we can rarely seem to agree on what "love" actually means.

I (Dave) wrote a book called, *The Seven Laws of Love: Essential Principles for Building Stronger Relationships,* where I started by looking at everything the Bible (the ultimate love and relationship manual) has to say on the subject.

Here are some of the most famous words ever written about love. Within in them, God is giving us a timeless roadmap for building stronger relationships. Below are seven very simple and practical ways to put these words into action in our daily lives how they could transform your marriage in the process.

"Love is patient and kind. Love is not jealous or boastful or proud or rude. It does not demand its own way. It is not irritable, and it keeps no record of being wronged.
It does not rejoice about injustice but rejoices whenever the truth wins out. Love never gives up, never loses faith, is always hopeful, and endures through every circumstance."
1 Corinthians 13:4-7

Here's how we put love into practice in marriage (it's simpler than you might think):

1. Love is patient, so in our rushed world, be patient with your spouse.
2. Love is kind, so in our sarcastic and often rude world, show genuine kindness to your spouse.
3. Love is not jealous or proud, so in our self-focused world, put the needs of your spouse ahead of your own.
4. Love keeps no record of wrongs, so in our world full of grudges and bitterness, choose to offer grace to your spouse.
5. Love rejoices in the truth, so in our world of dishonesty, always tell the truth and fight for trust in your marriage.
6. Love never loses faith, so in our world of skeptics and cynics, chose to believe the best about your spouse.
7. Love endures through every circumstance, so in our world of quitters, stay committed and never give up on your spouse! A "perfect marriage" is just two imperfect people who refuse to give up on each other.

HOW TO BUILD MORE TRUST IN
YOUR MARRIAGE

I (Ashley) hate to admit it, but I have, on more than one occasion, watched the once popular reality show "Cheaters." Every time I watch this show, I think about why spouses trust one another. And, how can we build more trust into our relationship?

For those who have kept your standards higher for your television viewing pleasure and aren't familiar with the show, the title really captures the essence and class of the program.

The show features a broken relationship in which one partner suspects the other of cheating so he or she goes to the "Cheaters" team for help in launching an all out private investigation with video footage, pictures, phone calls, and lots of trashy, uh, I mean classy drama. I feel sick the whole time I am watching these people spy on the suspect and the fights that ensue, but I just can't look away (not a proud moment).

In the end, the "Cheaters" team does in fact report the suspect as a cheater and the other partner is devastated. Tragically, their insecurity is proven to be justified. So, how can married couples keep this from happening?

The scenarios in this show are pretty outrageous because the producers want to attract viewers, but I believe that insecurity, founded AND unfounded, is destroying relationships, especially marriages. Everything we watch on television leaves us prone to question someone's motives or actions, even the ones we love most.

Have you ever found yourself driving around random parking lots looking for your spouse's car or even going through his or her phone without your spouse knowing? Have you caught your spouse looking frantically through your things or showing up at places that you frequent? Both situations involve a lack of trust that is rooted in the feeling of insecurity.

These feelings may have developed over time due to a spouse's continued pattern of cheating and lying, or you may generally be very hesitant to trust anyone due to past hurts that do not involve your spouse at all.

Regardless of the circumstances, feelings of insecurity and a lack of trust from either spouse are toxic in a marriage, and they must be addressed and dealt with as soon as possible.

In order for both partners to trust one another in the marriage, we not only need to remain faithful to our spouse (hence, the marital vows), but we also need to remove any barriers in our life that might make our spouse even question if we are worthy of his or her trust.

So, what does that look like? Here are five ways that you can build more trust in your marriage (in no particular order).

1. Answer the phone whenever your spouse calls.

This may be easier for some and harder for others due to work responsibilities (or, if you are like me, you don't hear it ring because you forgot it was on vibrate), but it is a simple way to improve the communication in your marriage.

Don't ignore your spouse's calls! If you can't answer right when he calls, send him a quick text to let him know that you saw the call and will call back when you have the chance. This keeps the line of communication open and is a kind and courteous way to build feelings of security in your marriage.

2. Get off the phone or computer when you are with your spouse.

For most of us, including Dave and myself, this is harder than it seems. We use our smartphones to chat with our loved ones, check social media, and even read our Bibles, all good things, but we still need to put our devices down when we are with our spouses, as much as we possibly can.

When we give our spouse our full attention, which means, "giving them our eyes and ears" (yes, just like your teacher would say), we are showing them that they are more important than whatever else is on the other side of that screen. This instills a feeling of security and helps us to be better listeners. We also need to do away with any passwords or devices that our spouse is unaware of. Nothing destroys trust more than secrets.

3. Watch where your eyes wander.

"But I say, anyone who looks at a woman with lust has already
committed adultery with her in his heart."
Matthew 5:28

Let's face it. We are going to notice an attractive person walking by, and that is okay. We can't cover our eyes in public places, but we can control the amount of time and thought we give to each glance. Let me be specific, when you see that hottie walking by, your eyes don't need to inspect them top to bottom or follow them to where they are going.

When we are constantly staring at other men or women, or if we make sly comments about how "cute" or "fit" or "pretty" someone else is, we are weakening the trust in our marriage. You might be telling yourself that this is harmless or innocent simply because you aren't having a physical affair with that person.

This is a dangerous lie because when we let our glances become lasting glances, lasting glances turn into thoughts, thoughts become fantasies, and fantasies, outside of your own spouse, destroy a marriage.

4. Say what you mean, and keep your word through your actions.

Trust is built through our consistent words and actions over time. So, we must be intentional about saying what we mean and keeping our word to our spouse. And, this is important with little every day things and big things.

No matter the circumstance, we must do our very best to follow through with what we have promised to our spouse on a consistent basis, both inside and outside of our home. The more we do this, the more trust we will have in our relationship.

5. Keep God as the center of your relationship.

"A person standing alone can be attacked and defeated, but two can stand back-to-back and conquer. Three are even better, for a triple-braided cord is not easily broken."
Ecclesiastes 4:12 NLT

I honestly never thought much about this verse until Dave and I had our premarital counseling. After one of our sessions, our pastor gave us a rather unusual wedding gift. He handed us a real "triple-braided cord." He then explained the verse and said that this illustrated a strong marriage in which the husband, wife and God each represent a strand of the cord, with God being the heartiest strand.

This kind of cord is hard to break and extremely secure, but the cord as a whole is only as strong as each strand. If one strand is compromised or cut off, the cord looses some of its strength and with enough weight it will eventually fold or break down completely.

The longer I am married and work with married couples, the more I see the truth of this verse played out. I am not sure where you might be in your faith, but I encourage you to make and keep God at the center of your marriage. So, how do we keep God as the primary "strand" in our marriage?

We do this by making our personal relationship with Christ a priority. We strive to know him more by going to church and reading our Bibles, and we make prayer a consistent part of our daily lives. When we keep our relationship with God as our top priority, our mind and hearts are more prepared to approach our spouse with the love and devotion he or she deserves, and we essentially keep our strands connected to the "master strand" and our "cord," or marriage, remains stronger.

OUR ALL-TIME FAVORITE MARRIAGE ADVICE

When we got married sixteen years ago, we were young and in love, but we were also pretty clueless! Along the way, we've had so many people share wise advice and life experiences with us, which helped to guide our family through good times and hard times. Through the years, we've been collecting some of the best marriage advice others have shared with us (and some we had to learn through our own mistakes).

If you'll apply these twenty-five principles below to your relationship, it could make a life-changing difference in your marriage! These timeless truths have changed our marriage for the better and they could change yours too.

1. Choose to love each other even in those moments when you struggle to like each other. Love is a commitment, not a feeling.
2. Always answer the phone when your husband/wife is calling and when possible, try to keep your phone off when you're together with your spouse.
3. Make time together a priority. Budget for a consistent date

night. Time is the "currency of relationships" so consistently invest time into your marriage.

4. Surround yourself with friends who will strengthen your marriage and remove yourself from people who may tempt you to compromise your character.

5. Make laughter the soundtrack of your marriage. Share moments of joy, and even in the hard times, find reasons to laugh.

6. In every argument, remember that there won't be a "winner" and a "loser." You are partners in everything so you'll either win together or lose together. Work together to find a solution.

7. Remember that a strong marriage rarely has two strong people at the same time. It's usually a husband and wife taking turns being strong for each other in the moments when the other feels weak.

8. Prioritize what happens in the bedroom. It takes more than sex to build a strong marriage, but it's nearly impossible to build a strong marriage without it!

9. Remember that marriage isn't 50-50; divorce is 50-50. Marriage has to be 100-100. It's not splitting everything in half, but both partners giving everything they've got!

10. Give your best to each other, not your leftovers after you've given your best to everyone else.

11. Learn from other people, but don't feel the need to compare your life or your marriage to anyone else's. God's plan for your life is masterfully unique!

12. Don't put your marriage on hold while you're raising your kids or else you'll end up with an empty nest and an empty marriage.

13. Never keep secrets from each other. Secrecy is the enemy of intimacy.

14. Never lie to each other. Lies break trust and trust is the foundation of a strong marriage.

15. When you've made a mistake, admit it and humbly seek

forgiveness. You should be quick to say, *"I was wrong. I'm sorry. Please forgive me."*

16. When your husband/wife breaks your trust give them your forgiveness instantly which will promote healing and create the opportunity for trust to be rebuilt. You should be quick to say, *"I love you. I forgive you. Let's move forward."*

17. Be patient with each other. Your spouse is always more important that your schedule.

18. Model the kind of marriage that will make your sons want to grow up to be good husbands and your daughters want to grow up to be good wives.

19. Be your spouse's biggest encourager, not his or her biggest critic. Be the one who wipes away their tears, not the one who causes them.

20. Never talk badly about your spouse to other people or vent about them online. Protect your spouse at all times and in all places.

21. Always wear your wedding ring. It will remind you that you're always connected to your spouse and it will remind the rest of the world that you're off limits!

22. Connect into a community of faith. A good church can make a world of difference in your marriage and family.

23. Pray together. Every marriage is stronger with God in the middle of it. A Christ-centered marriage is a healthy marriage.

24. When you have to choose between saying nothing or saying something mean to your spouse, say nothing every time!

25. Never consider divorce as an option. Remember that a "perfect marriage" is just two imperfect people who refuse to give up on each other!

YOUR SECOND HONEYMOON

In this final chapter, we want to challenge you to implement the new habits you've learned. It's really our habits that make a marriage. We also want to help you kick-start a second honeymoon of sorts by a romantic exchange of love letters and a vow renewal.

You might be thinking that this sounds corny, but stick with us for just a minute. It might renew some passion and have you chasing each other around the bedroom like a couple of newlyweds!

When was the last time you wrote a "love letter" to your spouse? When we lead marriage retreats and events, one exercise we always include involves each husband and wife writing a love letter to each other. When we explain the exercise, some people roll their eyes as if their inner dialogue is saying, "This is so cheesy! I haven't written a love letter since middle school."

We assure them that they need to trust us and this exercise will be well worth the effort. We remind them that our words have such power, and when we use our words to encourage and adore our spouses, our words can instantly improve intimacy in our marriages.

We instruct them to not just say, "I love you," but to write specific attributes they love about each other. We encourage them to share their feelings as honestly and specifically as they can.

Near the end of our time together, we have the couples each go to a place on the property where they can have some privacy and then take turns reading the letters to each other. At the end of their time of sharing, we encourage them to hold hands and pray together.

During the prayer, they should thank God for each other, pray about their dreams and hopes for the marriage, confess any negative behavior they need to change and recommit their lives to God and to each other.

After the "Love Letter Exercise" is completed, the couples return to the group and share. Many of them who had rolled their eyes before the exercise began now had tears in their eyes. We've had numerous couples tell us that the exercise was one of the most significant milestones in their marriage and the love letter from their spouse would be one of their most treasured possessions on earth.

Each time we lead couples through this time of sharing and see the impact their words can make on one another, we're reminded that words can shape a marriage. Your words, spoken with thoughtfulness, tenderness and love have immense power.

Use your words to build your spouse up, not to tear him or her down. Use your words to be your spouse's biggest encourager, not his or her biggest critic.

In every interaction with your spouse, live out the command of Ephesians 4:29 which says,

"Do not let any unwholesome talk come out of your mouths, but only what is helpful for building others up according to their needs, that it may benefit those who listen."

Creating a milestone moment in your marriage

In this final chapter, we want to give you the opportunity to experience a milestone moment with your spouse. It's going to require some thought and preparation on your part, but I promise, it will be well worth the effort! We'll begin with the Love Letter Exercise and then lead into a time of renewing your vows and then making a renewed promise of recommitment to each other.

The first step is to take time to write a letter to each other. You can type and print it out if necessary, but I encourage you to write the letter in your own handwriting. We've found that handwritten letters have become so rare in our culture, that when we do receive them (especially from a spouse), they are more likely to become a keepsake. We believe your spouse will treasure your letter for years to come!

Once you've both written the letter, choose a time and place to sit down and take turns reading them. While your spouse is reading, let them finish before you respond to their words. End the exercise by sharing your thoughts and feelings with each other and then transitioning into the renewing of your vows.

Renewing the Vows

Now that you've made it to the end of this journey, you hopefully have a renewed understanding of the six promises that will make or break a marriage. I encourage you to repeat these words to each other as a way to recommit your lives to each other and begin a new season of growth in your marriage.

Before you exchange these words, let's start with a quick recap of what each of the vows really means.

I Take You to be my Husband/Wife

In the entire world, you could only give this gift of your love to one person. You have chosen your spouse and they have chosen you! Never lose sight of this beautiful exchange. Be the best husband or wife you can be for them.

To Love and to Cherish

God calls husbands and wives to adore each other and to pursue each other with an ever-growing love. This is a commitment to invest in the friendship that sets the foundation for romantic love. It means to be creatively, thoughtfully and passionately working to win the heart of your spouse over and over again.

For Better or For Worse

You've got to love each other NO MATTER WHAT. Marital love can't be based on convenience or even feelings. This commitment means that our love will never be based on our circumstances. Your vows are most important in the moments when they are least convenient.

In Sickness or in Health

You can't always control what happens to your health, but you can always control how you choose to respond. Recommit to loving and supporting each other completely in moments of health, but also in moments of injury or illness.

Forsaking All Others

Marriage must remain monogamous. Refuse to allow anyone else to steal your spouse's rightful place in your mind, your heart or your bed. Recommit to loving each other with wholehearted fidelity and devotion.

For Richer or For Poorer

Commit to each other that money will never be your primary pursuit. Your love has nothing to do with whether you're bankrupt or wealthy. Money comes and money goes, but your commitment to each other must stand firm.

Once you've had a moment to reflect upon the significance of the vows and the journey you've taken up to this point, please take your spouse's hand and repeat these sacred promises to each other:

. . .

"I _____, take you _____, to be my husband/wife. To love and to cherish, for better or for worse, for richer or for poorer, in sickness or in health, forsaking all others, 'til death do us part!"

YOU MAY NOW KISS the bride! Now, run to the bedroom and make love like it's your wedding night!

Congratulations! You've come to the end of this journey, but it's really much more of a starting point than a finish line. We hope this book has helped you refuel your relationship and refocus your resolve as you look to the road ahead.

We pray God's continued blessings and guidance for you both through all the celebrations and challenges of life. If you'll continue to walk through life hand-in-hand, trusting God and supporting each other, there's nothing that can come between you!

Dave & Ashley Willis

AN EXCLUSIVE EXCERPT OF THE NAKED MARRIAGE

Click To Buy Now
The Naked Marriage

NAKED IS GOOD

Dave

I remember it like it was yesterday. I had just returned home for summer break and I was starting work at a camp before heading back to college for my senior year. Ashley and I had been talking about marriage since our third date, and the time had come to get the ring and plan a perfect evening to propose. I wanted to close the deal fast before she realized that she was way out of my league and could probably find a much better guy if she looked around.

With the help of her parents, I planned an elaborate story to give me an excuse to go and do some prep work. I told her that I needed to go visit my brother who had just broken his collarbone. I hadn't thought through my backstory well because she said she wanted to come with me, so in a panic, I blurted out, "You can't…he's naked!"

"What? Why is he naked?"—she was shocked.

"I don't know. When he's injured, he likes to be naked! I know, it's weird, but you can't come. He wouldn't want you to see him like that," I awkwardly blurted.

Ashley was disappointed and confused when I left. I had knots in my stomach from nervousness and from the guilt of just having told her a ridiculous lie. To this day, I'm terrible at lying to her, which has worked out great for our marriage.

Finally, I made it back to take her to dinner and everything was ready. She looked stunning in a red dress that brought out the beautiful tones of her strawberry-blonde hair. I kept thinking, *No way is she going to say yes. She is way out of my league!*

We went out to the nicest restaurant in town, and I paid a small fortune for a meal that I was too nervous to eat. We finally made it to the spot where I was going to pop the question. It was a place called Ashland, and the weather and scenery were beautiful. My hands were shaking as I pulled out a handwritten letter and began reading it to her. I professed my undying love and commitment to her, and I promised to always love and cherish her and to build our future on a foundation of faith in God. I got down on one knee and asked her to spend her life with me. She took a deep breath and exclaimed, "No way!" My heart sank, until I realized that it was a good "no way", and she hugged me and said, "Yes!" It was one of the happiest moments of my life and it began a journey that led us to our wedding.

We had planned a beautiful day, gone through premarital counseling, and prayed that God would bless our marriage. We were completely prepared, right? Well, in some ways, yes. In other ways—absolutely not. There are many things that I wish someone would have told us before our wedding day. You know…the real stuff. The stuff they don't talk about in premarital class at church—the *inside* scoop.

Now that we have been married for nearly twenty years, what would we say to that bright-eyed, wonder-filled, young couple in love? (Our younger selves thought we knew everything about marriage.) I think I would tell them that marriage is more complex than they realize. We wanted to be the perfect couple, but our illusions about perfection were unrealistic. We soon discovered that God's definition of a healthy marriage is often different from what we see in the world around us, because a healthy marriage is a *naked marriage*.

One of the first love lessons Ashley and I learned in our marriage was the power of a naked marriage. You probably think I'm just talking about sex right now, but there's a lot more to it than that. The sexual aspect of your marriage should be a huge priority, but true intimacy requires more than just what happens in the bedroom.

Ashley

Dave and I are passionate about what we call the *naked marriage*, but we didn't come up with this idea. God did. Not only is God passionate about marriage, but the Bible has a lot to say about marriage too. In fact, the Bible begins with a marriage—*Adam and Eve*.

In Genesis, God paints a picture of this perfect place called Eden. Here, God created Adam and Eve in His own image and they were together—it was *paradise*. "Now the man and his wife were both naked, but they felt no shame" (Genesis 2:25, NLT). This was before sin and all the baggage entered the scene. And just for a beautiful moment, we got this picture of what marriage could be—intimate, open, honest, vulnerable, and loving.

God created a couple who temporarily lived in an ideal setting with no debt, no crazy in-laws, no baggage, no stress, no fighting, and finally—no clothing! Dave likes to say, "They didn't have anything up their sleeves, because they weren't wearing any sleeves!" This first married couple was intimately connected, and they had each other's back. They were strengthened by each other's love, and their relationship was built on a solid foundation of commitment—commitment to each other and to God.

The secret-free marriage, or the *naked marriage*, is a beautiful picture of what God wants our relationship with Him to look like. Unfortunately, we live in a world where we receive conflicting pictures of what marriage is supposed to be. From the time we are little, we are bombarded with ideas and opinions of marriage.

Whether it's about sex or emotional intimacy and connection, many of us struggle with feeling vulnerable, but that is what God intended—for marriage to be naked. The fear of intimacy is normal. We all carry this fear: *Am I lovable, am I worthy, would they still want me if they saw the whole me?*

Every couple wonders if they can be completely naked spiritually, emotionally, and physically. Many times, it's hard to verbalize what we like and don't like about how marriage looks, so couples are left feeling confused. When this happens, the picture of marriage starts to feel more complicated. Society continues this notion of entering marriage clueless because we are told, "It's really not about the marriage, it's about the wedding." And so, couples put all their time and resources into preparing for the wedding, but they don't give time to planning for a successful marriage. We need to enter marriage asking, "What is it really supposed to look like?"

Perhaps you look to your own parents and your own family. You may like some of the things your parents did, but maybe you have some things you want to do differently. Your spouse may also have their own ideas because of the influence of their parents.

Dave and I came from very different backgrounds. Because of what we experienced growing up, going into our marriage we had different ideas of sex and intimacy. Dave grew up in a home where his parents were always flirting with each other and being silly, and his mom was always sitting on her husband's lap, and they would hold hands. They were affectionate with one another.

While I grew up in a loving home where my parents cared about each other deeply, they were not openly affectionate with one another and they never talked to us about sex. If sex was ever mentioned it was in the context of, "Dear God! Never do it!" Actually, my wedding day was the first time my mom was willing to bring up the topic of sex. I was twenty years old when Dave and I got married and right before our ceremony, my mom looked over at me and said for the *first* time, "Well, I guess we better talk about sex." I told her it was a little late for that, because by this point what I knew about sex was through friends and health class.

Going into our marriage, Dave and I waited to have sex, but I built up my expectations of what sex was supposed to be (or not be), and I was anxious and scared. Even after having a great wedding night, I still had a lot of apprehensions about sex, and I didn't feel like I knew what I was doing. Then my anxieties were amplified when I discovered, early in our marriage, that Dave had been looking at porn. And while he quickly repented and began to rebuild trust, I still felt fearful and awkward about sex. Originally, I thought this part of our relationship would be easy and just work itself out, so I was surprised when at first it didn't. To make matters worse, I didn't always share with Dave how I was feeling, but when I discovered Dave's porn struggle, we started talking about what was going on in our lives and about our expectations.

We did have fear of intimacy and vulnerability early in our marriage, but as Dave and I travel and talk to couples, we've discovered that we aren't alone. Even if trust has been broken in your marriage, you can rebuild it. Even if you have the same hang-ups and insecurities that Dave and I had, being vulnerable (as hard as that is) is only going to help your marriage to grow closer.

Dave

Do you remember the first time you told your spouse, "I love you!"—I do. That special day is vivid in my mind...for more reasons than one.

To accurately paint the picture of this scene, you need to know it was one of the least romantic places imaginable: my dingy, dirty college dorm room. To my knowledge, my roommate hadn't washed his sheets even once in the two years I'd been living with him. We constantly sprayed Febreze and Lysol, but our best efforts to mask the stench of dirty clothes, wet towels, and old food did little to create much ambience.

My sweet mom nearly cried the first time she visited. As unpleasant as the surroundings may have been, all those unsavory details seemed to disappear when I looked at Ashley. I had never felt that way about anyone, and I figured it had to be love. I had to tell her. It felt like a volcano of unexpressed emotion was welling up in my heart and trying to come out of my mouth. I knew that if I didn't say something right then, there was a decent chance I'd end up puking on her instead. This was a defining moment and the first time I was truly vulnerable.

The look on my face must have been a combination of nausea, fear, anticipation, confusion, and joy. Ashley gave me a concerned look with those gorgeous eyes of hers and said, "What are you thinking about?"

I felt completely vulnerable and exposed, like I was standing in my underwear in front of everyone I knew. And just to be clear, I've never looked very attractive in my underwear. (The more of my body I can cover up, the more attractive it seems.) My mouth was dry, and I was having trouble forming coherent words, but I swallowed hard and gathered my strength. And with the squeaky voice of a prepubescent adolescent, I finally said, "I was thinking...I was thinking that I love you."

I got it out. It was not one of my smoothest moments, and I doubt the scene will ever be replayed in a great love story, but I got it out. I said it. She smiled at me, and without hesitation she said, "I love you too." Even though we were still in my nasty dorm room, in that moment we might as well have been on top of the Eiffel Tower with fireworks going off in the background. I had expressed my love, and that love had been reciprocated. It's amazing how free and how strong you can feel when you are completely vulnerable, and you receive *love* in exchange.

Through our years together and the different seasons of our marriage and family, our love and vulnerability has grown deeper and richer. We've gained a fuller understanding of what vulnerability really means. But vulnerability is not something that is defined by words alone. It is our choice each day to live without secrets. To live completely honest and open with our spouse—naked in every way. Everything changes for the better in our marriages when we are committed to being vulnerable with each other and *secret free*.

Ashley

A secret-free relationship creates a solid foundation of commitment—commitment to each other and to God. During premarital counseling, our pastor opened his Bible and read,

"A person standing alone can be attacked and defeated, but two can stand back-to-back and conquer. Three are even better, for a triple-braided cord is not easily broken"
Ecclesiastes 4:12 (NLT)

Up until that moment, I honestly never thought much about this verse, but after one of our sessions, our pastor gave us a rather unusual wedding gift. He handed us a real triple-braided cord.

He then explained the verse and said that this illustrated a strong marriage in which the husband, wife, and God each represent a strand of the cord, with God being the heartiest strand. This kind of cord is hard to break and extremely secure, but the cord is only as strong as each strand. If one strand is weakened or cut off, the cord loses some of its strength and with enough weight it will eventually fray and break down completely.

The longer we are married and work with married couples, the more we see the truth of this verse played out. I am not sure where you might be in your faith, but I encourage you to keep God at the center of your marriage. How do we keep God as the primary *strand* in our marriage? We do this by making our personal relationship with Christ a priority. We strive to know Him more by going to church and reading our Bibles, and we make prayer a consistent part of our daily lives. When we keep our relationship with God as our top priority, our minds and hearts are more prepared to approach our spouse with the love and devotion he or she deserves, and we essentially keep our strands connected to the master strand. When this happens, our *cords* of marriage remain strong.

When God painted this picture of a *naked marriage*, He was revealing to us something more than just sexual intimacy; He was revealing the importance of having complete transparency, vulnerability, acceptance, and intimacy at every level of the relationship. I'm certainly not advocating that we all walk around naked all day (although Dave and I do think most marriages would benefit from more naked time), but I am suggesting that we all need to become more intentional about reconnecting with that true intimacy that Adam and Eve got a taste of in the Garden of Eden. Marital love has to be completely open, honest, and transparent. Secrets are as dangerous as lies and can rob your relationship of intimacy and trust. Love, by its very nature, *is* honest, and this is especially important to the sacred bond of trust in marriage.

Through our years together and the different seasons of our marriage and family, our love has grown deeper and richer. We've also gained a fuller understanding of what marriage really means. It's not something that can be defined by feelings or captured by words alone. God created marriage to be a transformative force in every aspect of our lives, and once we understand and embrace it, our marriage will come into clearer focus and will grow in deeper levels of intimacy and vulnerability.

Dave

Ashley and I interact with thousands of couples and we see a trend of marriages ending because of *incompatibility*. There's a huge modern myth that divorce due to *incompatibility* will solve all the problems you're facing in your marriage, but the reality is, divorce usually creates more problems than it solves. Instead of committing to the covenant of marriage, more and more couples choose to end it. It's not that there's anything wrong with marriage. In fact, marriage is more important than ever. The problem is our modern culture has taken this beautiful gift of marriage and gone about it in the wrong way. We're missing the point of marriage, and families are being built without a solid foundation.

Why are fewer people choosing to marry when studies consistently show that marriages reduce crime, give increased stability to children, increase life expectancy, increase emotional happiness, and produce more wealth? The temptation and anxiety associated with marriage is so strong these days that people are afraid to make the commitment and more and more people simply choose to stay single. But God created marriage to be much more than cohabitating; it's a covenant. We need to build marriage upon our commitments. The strongest couples have learned that marriage means choosing to love each other even on those days when you struggle to like each other. When both spouses commit to be vulnerable and secret free, the marriage thrives.

Ashley

Often, we tend to think that all marriage problems stem from a big breach of trust. However, many times the lack of love isn't because of a one-time sin but an ongoing pattern of behavior leading to what Dave and I call a "cable-company marriage." I know that probably sounds pretty random, so let me explain.

Have you ever noticed how cable companies treat their customers with amazing care and attentiveness when they're first trying to seal the deal? However, once they've got you, the introductory rates are replaced with much more expensive rates and the customer service takes a nosedive, which makes you want to trade in your old cable company for a new one. The cable TV industry seems focused on a model of treating people really well at first but then taking them for granted in the long run.

Sadly, a lot of marriages operate this way too. In the beginning, when the couple is trying to win each other's hearts, they roll out the red carpet. They give the very best of themselves, but it doesn't last long. Once the day-to-day reality of life together sets in, they stop doing all those things they did in the beginning. They take each other for granted, and it isn't long before they both start longing for something new where they'll be treated well again.

It doesn't have to be this way! Marriages should grow stronger with time. Couples should continue pursuing, encouraging, and loving each other through all the seasons of the relationship.

If you find yourself in a cable-company marriage right now, don't lose hope. Don't throw away your relationship just to start a new one with someone else and repeat the same cycle. Make a commitment to transform your marriage. Stop taking each other for granted. Your best days together can still be ahead of you and not behind you.

Dave and I have discovered that being married is more complex than we naively assumed it would be in the beginning. We both had a desire to become a perfect spouse, but we soon discovered that God's definition of a healthy marriage is often different from what we see in the world around us. We all have in our minds what a perfect marriage looks like, but a marriage where there is commitment and vulnerability is the *best* kind.

The beauty of a *naked marriage* happens when a husband and wife live with complete vulnerability, transparency, and trust. That's the way God intended marriage when He made the first couple "naked and unashamed." And though you probably shouldn't be naked in public, unless you'd like to get an arrest and some awkward posts about you on social media, God still wants us to have naked marriages today. It is our hope and prayer that as you and your spouse read these pages, you both will discover how to make His presence more profound in your relationship, and that you'll learn the beautiful truth that a perfect marriage—a naked marriage—is just two imperfect people who refuse to give up on each other.

Dave

In the *naked marriage*, everything changes for the better. But before that can happen, there must be commitment to vulnerability and to *nakedness* in every way. Without real vulnerability and honesty, there can be no real love.

One year, our kids had an ongoing project of building a fort in the empty lot next to our house. Almost every day after school, they would meet up with the other neighborhood kids and look for scrap materials to add to their beloved masterpiece. It was really nothing more than some old crates and cardboard stacked together. Every time a storm came, the whole thing fell apart, and they would start the whole process over again.

I've never been much help on the fort project because I'm terrible with tools. Ashley's dad is a guy who can build and fix anything, so when Ashley married me, she assumed all men had the same skill set. I wish I had those skills, but when I try swinging a hammer, stuff gets broken. Ashley is both the beautiful one and the handy one in our relationship.

The boys wish I was better at construction so I could help them build forts. I do my best to help them gather materials, but my most valuable contribution thus far has been a single bit of engineering advice. I told them the fort was going to keep collapsing until they built it securely on a solid foundation.

Many marriages resemble that old fort. Maybe there's a lot of effort going into building the marriage, but it still seems to struggle—seemingly falling apart. Some marriages fall apart due to a lack of effort, but many more marriages fail for the same reasons the boys' fort kept collapsing. The husband and wife built their relationship with the wrong tools and with no solid foundation.

Matthew 7:24–27 contains one of Jesus' most famous teachings. He tells the story of a wise builder and a foolish builder. This wise builder took the time to build his house on a foundation of solid rock, while the foolish builder took the fast and easy route and built his house on sand.

From the outside, both houses looked the same, but the difference was revealed when a storm came. The strong winds and rains beat against both houses, and the house without a solid foundation collapsed. The house built on the rock stood strong.

When you read magazines and look at the examples of marriages in pop culture, it seems as though many people are content to build a marriage with no solid foundation. These shaky marriages are usually based on fickle feelings, codependent insecurities, mutual convenience or lust. When the storms of life come, the marriage can't survive.

Feelings are real, but we should never let them rule us. When we build our marriage on our feelings instead of our commitment, the marriage will be shaky at best because there was no solid foundation. There's nothing wrong with feelings. They're an important part of life, but they were never intended to be our compass or our *foundation*. Feelings are fickle.

The strongest marriages, however, are built on a foundation of love, vulnerability, and commitment. The strength of your commitment will always determine the strength of your marriage. God's definition of marriage is rooted in the concept of commitment and vulnerability. When you said, "I do," to your spouse, you weren't just expressing your current feelings; you were making a promise of commitment that will ultimately be your legacy of love.

Marriage, by its very nature, is a conscious choice to selflessly put the needs of your spouse ahead of your own preferences or comforts. No marriage can survive unless it is rooted in rock-solid commitment and honest vulnerability.

As a pastor for many years, I had the privilege of officiating wedding ceremonies. It's such an honor to stand in that sacred moment with a bride and groom as they exchange vows and rings and enter into the holy covenant of marriage. One of the Bible passages I often read at wedding ceremonies comes from Ruth 1:16–17:

> *But Ruth replied, "Don't ask me to leave you and turn back.*
> *Wherever you go, I will go; wherever you live, I will live. Your people*
> *will be my people, and your God will be my God. Wherever you die, I*
> *will die, and there I will be buried. May the Lord punish me severely*
> *if I allow anything but death to separate us!" (NLT)*

These words beautifully capture the commitment necessary for a strong marriage. God wants to create a generational impact through your marriage. The level at which your marriage will make an eternal impact is defined by your level of commitment to pursuing and possessing a *naked marriage*. There is no relationship more sacred than your marriage, so treasure your spouse. Never let anyone or anything take the place of priority your spouse should hold in your heart. Marriage is one of God's greatest gifts.

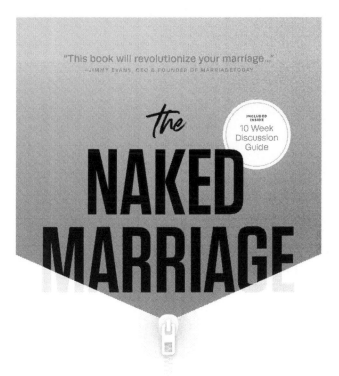

"This book will revolutionize your marriage..."
—JIMMY EVANS, CEO & FOUNDER OF MARRIAGETODAY

the

NAKED MARRIAGE

INCLUDED INSIDE
10 Week Discussion Guide

Undressing the truth about sex,
intimacy and lifelong love

DAVE & ASHLEY WILLIS

AUTHORS OF 7 DAYS TO A STRONGER MARRIAGE

The Naked Marriage

Also by Dave & Ashley
Imagine a marriage with amazing sex, but where great sex is only the
icing on the cake.

ABOUT THE AUTHORS

Dave and Ashley Willis have become two of America's most trusted voices on issues related to marriage, faith and family. They are part of the team at MarriageToday which is the nation's largest marriage ministry. Dave and Ashley's videos, articles, books, podcasts and live events reach millions of couples worldwide. They live with their four young sons near Dallas, TX. For additional resources, please visit MarriageToday.com

Printed in Great Britain
by Amazon

54385113R00099